MW00988457

TESTIMONIALS

AUG 1 4 2011

D R Toi
223 Southlake Pl
Newport News VA 23602-8323

8 - 21 - 2011

Ann:

Your book is a fascinating journey through many dreams about UFOs, meetings with contactees, work with astronomer J. Allen Hynek, and the strange world in which we live

Stanton Friedman, nuclear physicist

Ann's open heart manner, her impersonal honesty, and her personal knowledge gave us the opportunity to accept her as a powerful ally and professional advocate.

She was able to speak to those who focus on the physical level, the biological level, the psychosocial level, and the spiritual level of UFO/ET phenomena. And she wowed the crowd with her assertive comments about governmental secrecy and the cover-up of the ET Presence."

R Leo Sprinkle, Ph.D.
Professor Emeritus, University of Wyoming
UFO Researcher

"Ann, you are dealing with the subject of Disclosure; be prepared... many people will try to block your valuable information or discredit you. This is an ambitious project. You are an extraordinary person and I greatly admire your courage and determination."

Carol Adler, MFA
Author and President, Dandelion Enterprises, Inc.
http://www.write-to-publish-for-profit.com

Ann weaves a beautiful tapestry of her interesting life. Her devotion to the work of UFO researcher and respected astronomer J Allen Hynek is part of this biographical work of art. It is definitely worth reading.

Paola Leopizzi Harris
Author, *Exopolitics: All The Above*

Ann woke me up to the possibility of contact between an individu like myself and an intelligent being from another world. I have found her to always be honest and open to the truth as it presented itself to her. She is highly spiritual and a great friend to me, her Sisters and to off-world visitors and she has a story to share.

Wayne Peterson
Software Engineer
UFO/ETI Researcher

DRAGON IN THE SKY

Prophecy From the Stars

by Ann Eller

THE BOOK TREE

San Diego, California

© 2010 Ann Eller

All rights reserved. No part of this book may be reproduced, transmitted or utilized in any form or by any means, electronic or mechanical, including photocopying, recording, scanning or by any information storage or retrieval system, without permission in writing from the author, except for brief quotations in articles, books and reviews.

ISBN 978-1-58509-135-5

Second Revised Edition

Dragon cover art
copyright by Sergey Mikhaylov

Cover layout and design
Atulya Berube

Published by
The Book Tree
P O Box 16476
San Diego, CA 92176
www.thebooktree.com

We provide fascinating and educational products to help awaken the public to new ideas and information that would not be available otherwise.
Call 1 (800) 700-8733 for our *FREE BOOK TREE CATALOG*.

THIS BOOK IS DEDICATED TO

The Ancient Sisterhood of Light

Table of Contents

ACKNOWLEDGMENTS

This book has had a long, very long period of gestation. During that time there have been those who have given it a boost and a bit of encouragement. I wish to thank them from the bottom of my heart for helping to make this message possible.

My dear friend Bee Boe who is always ready to lend a hand on the spur of the moment and continuously encouraging and staying positive.

Friends, Victoria and Chuck Oldham who saw the potential and offered real and solid advice and help.

To Jocelyn Buckner, many thanks, who helped put it all together and made it coherent. Without her, this would never have been completed.

To my loving family who at times thought I was going over the edge.

And to my friends and family from the stars who have watched over my shoulder and given the needed inspiration to make it all happen.

FOREWORD

It is a pleasure, Dear Reader, to introduce you to *DRAGON IN THE SKY: Prophecy from the Stars*, by Ann Eller RN NP.

Ann Eller has served so well in so many ways: Professional Nurse, UFO Investigator, Personal Assistant to Dr. J. Allen Hynek, PhD, (considered to have been the Dean of USA UFO Researchers), and as ET Experiencer.

Now, as Author and Messenger, Ann brings to us the summary of her life, her work, and her message.

Like most UFO Researchers, Ann is bright, educated, and competent in her investigative abilities and activities. She demonstrates a high level of curiosity, courage, and compassion in dealing with other persons who report interactions with Extraterrestrial and Interdimensional Entities.

When she came to the University of Wyoming, 1985, to participate in the Rocky Mountain Conference on UFO Investigation, she immediately gained many friends and colleagues, with her warm smile and her graceful enthusiasm. Her open heart manner, her impersonal honesty, and her personal knowledge gave us the opportunity to accept her as a powerful ally and professional advocate.

She was able to speak to those who focus on the physical level, the biological level, the psychosocial level, and the spiritual level of UFO/ET phenomena. And she wowed the crowd with her assertive comments about governmental secrecy and the cover-up of the ET Presence.

Now she shares with us her personal experiences, including behind-the-scenes information about Dr. Hynek and his research activities. She describes her own spiritual commitment and development; her service as a White House volunteer; and the messages from the Ancient Sisters of Light about Planet X, planetary changes on Earth, and the transformation of Humanity.

Ann Eller, as Author, has analyzed various scenarios that are occurring on Earth. Ann Eller, as Messenger, is stating that we should prepare for the coming changes: "It is time to graduate to a higher level of consciousness. Wake up!"

Welcome, Dear Reader. May we all learn from the views and the visions of Ann Eller. May we all ascend

In Love and Light,
R. Leo Sprinkle, Ph.D.
Author of *Soul Samples* (1999 Granite Publishing)
Counseling Psychologist
Professor Emeritus, University of Wyoming
UFO Researcher

PREFACE

During the time I was shopping this manuscript around, I received an answer from one publishing company asking me to remove the information about Planet X as it was " speculative-- but may be true. The inclusion may damage your books appeal, reduce your credibility and cut into sales."

If I removed all of Planet X they would be very interested in publishing the rest of the story.

Here is my reply:

Thank you for taking the time to read and honestly critique the manuscript of *DRAGON IN THE SKY: Prophecy from the Stars*. It is very helpful and you may be right that inclusion of Nibiru (Planet X) may damage my reputation and the book sales.

However, the message must stand as written. It is either truth or it is not. I believe Nibiru and the cataclysms of its passage are dead ahead! It is too late for this planet to change its course. Perhaps some time ago there was an opportunity to alter the events but it didn't happen.

My message is what I have "seen" and I must give it out as I have "seen" it.

I am well aware that some folks will not be able to handle the truth. But I believe Humanity has a right to know what is coming and the right to have an opportunity to prepare, to love more genuinely, to right the wrongs in their lives, and to be of help to others who will need us.

It will be a fantastic opportunity to grow spiritually.

Generally I agree with you that we create our own reality. This is true. However for an entire planet (which also creates its own reality) the population must be of one mind. Our Earth, in my lifetime, has NEVER achieved this feat. Currently we have more Souls attempting to change the negative than ever before in our recorded history. We are becoming much more conscious but we will not have reached critical mass before Nibiru passes.

I have always been a positive thinker. My Mother's mantra was from the song, " You've got to accentuate the positive---eliminate the negative---and don't mess with Mr. Inbetween."

I believe it is a very positive step to tell the people the truth. Give them a chance to survive, if they so desire, and give them the time to put their life in order and make peace with their own God.

This is the thrust of the message. Believe me, if I could wave a magic wand and turn Nibiru around and send it back to the outer edges of the galaxy, I would do it without hesitation.

The 5th world that the Ancient Native Americans foresaw is beautiful and peaceful and it will happen in time. However, in order to get there we must go through what is just up ahead.

Blessings,
Ann Eller

Since everything is but an apparition,

Perfect in being what it is,

Having nothing to do with good or bad,

Acceptance or rejection,

You might as well burst out laughing!

~ Longchenpa

Chapter 1

Dr. J. Allen Hynek and Me

My personal UFO alien experience begins with a letter about my dreams -- every night for four years I dreamt of UFOs.

I wrote to ufologist Dr. J. Allen Hynek in 1980, who at the time was enjoying continued kudos for his contributions as a scientific advisor on Steven Spielberg's Close Encounters of the Third Kind. (Dr. Hynek even made a brief cameo appearance near the end of the movie.) I truly identified with the main character, Roy Neary (played by Richard Dreyfuss) who, after UFO contact, becomes obsessed with the subject. After four years of dreaming about "the UFO problem," I felt like building Devil's Tower with my mashed potatoes too.

The UFO alien dreams were like a computer download. I awoke each morning with a feeling that I had been physically tapped on the head and imparted with a high level of knowledge. But the dreams haunted me through my waking hours and I could think of nothing else except the bug-eyed aliens with praying mantis arms, the black helicopters, secret underground military bases, and the alien presence around us.

I wrote to Dr. Hynek to ask about them, never realizing that I would one day become Hynek's personal assistant and attend a UFO conference in his stead. It was at that conference when I would experience the first of many encounters with aliens and spiritual guides – and they gave me a powerful message to share with the world.

I became interested in UFOs after reading a magazine article on the Betty and Barney Hill alien abduction story. Betty and Barney Hill's encounter was generally unknown to the public until 1966 when *Look* magazine published an excerpt of the best-selling book, *The Interrupted Journey*, by John G. Fuller. (This story was also made into a 1975 NBC-TV movie called "The UFO Incident.") The Hills revealed under hypnosis that they had been abducted, medically probed, and thoroughly traumatized by aliens from Zeta Reticuli. Deep down inside I just knew every word of Betty and Barney's story was true. At the end of the article the author wrote, "Fact or fiction – we must let the reader decide for himself."

I was incensed that anyone would think that the Hill story was a hoax. It was obvious to me that we are not alone in the universe.

This was the first documented case of its kind to be made public in the United States and I became riveted to the Hill's abduction experience in New Hampshire. Much later I began to read anything and everything about UFOs I could find. It was then that I discovered that every book, magazine or TV interview on the matter had a recurring name -- Dr. J. Allen Hynek.

Dr. Hynek was a scientific researcher of the highest integrity. He ranked number one in the "Who's Who" of UFO research and was fully committed to unraveling the true nature of the Unidentified Flying Objects. In the letter, I requested that he point me in the right direction if dreams were not his specialty. I'd later hear from him in a surprising manner.

Dr. Joseph Allen Hynek became involved in the UFO field as an astronomer. In 1948, the Air Force asked Hynek to look at the many reports on flying saucers that were coming in at the time. As a faculty member at Ohio State University, he was the astronomer closest to Dayton, Ohio - the location of the government's UFO project headquarters at Wright-Patterson Air Force Base (AFB). As a Professor of Astronomy, Hynek was asked to determine which of the UFO sightings resulted from misidentification of astronomical phenomena such as meteors, comets, planets, and stars. It wasn't long before Dr. Hynek became the scientific consultant to the Air Force and remained in that position for some twenty years.

Acting in his official capacity, Hynek was called to the scene of every major UFO sighting. In his early years Dr. Hynek was highly skeptical of extraterrestrial visitations, although by the end of his life, his view of UFOs would shift to the polar opposite.

Between the years 1952 and 1972, and having what was considered to be "impeccable credentials," Dr. J. Allen Hynek headed Project Blue Book, the top-secret investigation into UFOs for the military. Hynek was officially researching UFOs for the United States Air Force to compile the classified report.

A sudden up-tick in UFO sightings in the late 40s and early 50s and a good deal of media attention prompted a special Congressional hearing to review Project Bluebook. Dr. Hynek debated with a scientist's view about the "UFO problem" to the group. Following Hynek's lengthy disposition, Air Force General John Samford, who later was to become the Director of the National Security Agency, put on tap dancing shoes to announce that there were "credible observers of relatively incredible things." Neither Hynek nor Samford specifically denied that UFOs existed.

The Congressional hearing concluded that "the evidence presented on unidentified flying objects shows no indication that these phenomena constitute a threat to national security and the continued emphasis on the reporting of the phenomena does, in perilous times, result in a threat to the orderly function of the protective organs of the body politic." An Air Force directive to service personnel was established that prohibits talking about UFOs unless "it has been positively identified as a familiar or known object." In addition, a Joint Chiefs of Staff directive – JANAP 146B – threatens prosecution under the Espionage Act to military personnel, commercial pilots and merchant seamen who discuss any sightings in public.

It was decided to "strip the UFOs of the special status that they had been given and the aura of mystery they had acquired... national security was not endangered by the UFOs." But according to Hynek's colleagues, Blue Book could hardly have been expected to be effective while the "aura of mystery" continued, because of continued secrecy surrounding much of its activities. The secrecy simply made the UFO subject more interesting.

Project Blue Book was shelved (or went underground) in 1969 and UFO research was hushed. False explanations from Hynek and his military colleagues attributed sightings of saucers to (pick one) Swamp Gas, the Planet Venus, Sodium Vapor Clouds, Ball Lightning, some sort of psychological problem with the witness, or mass hysteria.

Dr. Hynek later confessed in a lecture to colleagues that some of the reports he studied were indeed "puzzling." He said, "I thought the whole thing was a question of post-war nerves. But there was persistence to the phenomena that refused to dry up and blow away. It finally led me to the belief that we had real phenomena to deal with."

As time passed, thousands of unexplained accounts by eyewitnesses had accumulated. Dr. Hynek, always the dedicated scientist, conceded there was just too much compelling evidence to be carelessly dismissed. Approximately 20 percent of the reports could not be explained away, and these reports eventually convinced Dr. Hynek that the UFO phenomenon needed more study.

People in the 1960s and early-70s did not come forward to report their UFO sightings and other high strangeness stories due to the "giggle-factor." The public had become shy; people were reluctant because too many had been mocked and life had been made miserable for them. Many witnesses – like Betty and Barney Hill – suffered ridicule, marital problems, and depression.

Founded in Chicago in 1972, the J. Allen Hynek Center for UFO Studies, or CUFOS, opened with the philosophy that witnesses could be anonymous and all sightings were worthy of investigation. In 1985, Hynek moved to Scottsdale, Arizona and started the International Center for UFO Research, or ICUFOR.

"Ridicule is not a part of the scientific method," J. Allen Hynek said, "and the public should not be taught that it is."

A few weeks after I had mailed the letter to Dr. J. Allen Hynek about my UFO dreams, I was disappointed that I had not received an answer. I finally stopped waiting after a month or so, and put the whole episode out of my mind.

It was in 1980 -- a full nine months after I had posted the letter -- when the phone rang. It was nine o'clock at night and I picked up.

A man's voice said, "May I speak with Ann Eller, please?"

I said, "Speaking."

"This is Dr. Hynek."

My stomach churned with the inertia of a quickly falling elevator making my head spin. I had to sit down.

"I apologize for not getting back to you sooner. I just found your letter behind my desk."

(During my time with the man, I learned that the good doctor was the epitome of the absent-minded professor and this behavior of finding an unopened piece of mail in an odd place was typical.)

He said, "I want you to know that I'm interested in your dreams. Tell me a little bit about them."

I could hardly concentrate, given the greatness of Dr. J. Allen Hynek who was, at that moment, at the other end of the line. But I told him about the constant dreams, night after night, of aliens, UFOs landing, spacecraft, other worlds with the different species, alien cultures, the underwater flying objects, men in military uniforms, black helicopters, secret bases and the high levels of government involvement.

He asked, "Do you have a log? Have you written them down?"

I said "yes," but I was thinking "sorta, kinda."

"I'm very interested in your case. Would you send me a copy of your dream log?"

"Yes, I'd be very happy to."

"I'll look forward to seeing them." Then he said, "Because it's a world-wide phenomenon... people all over the world report having these dreams."

I had an up-rush of energy as we hung up. I couldn't stop smiling as the famous Dr. Hynek's voice echoed in my every thought. I picked up the phone and called my dear friend, Bee.

I said, "Quick! I need you to help me put all of these dreams into a readable form."

Bee came over and we spent one whole evening putting these dream fragments together and sent them off to Hynek.

I included a letter asking him to refer me to anyone in Arizona I could ask about my UFO dream experiences. I also asked for his opinion of what these dreams might mean.

I wrote: "Can you please point me to someone, somewhere in Arizona I can talk to who can explain what these dreams are about?"

I later learned that these dreams would unlock the secrets of my UFO experiences.

Chapter 2

The Dream Log

Everyone should have a friend like Bee. She is of like-mind regarding any metaphysical subject -- but more importantly, when I phoned her she immediately came to my aid. Using her excellent secretarial skills, we sorted through scraps of paper, notebooks, and journals to create the dream log for Dr. Hynek.

The dreams had been constant; the UFO dreams had hindered my sleep nearly every night for four years. There were times when I walked around in a complete daze, haunted by the thoughts, images, and sensations I felt after having these lucid UFO dreams. Some nights, I awoke to a light-filled room. The brilliant light would vanish as soon as I became cognizant of it. Then I'd hear a swishing sound outside. I felt I had been somewhere else, somewhere other than my bed. Some dreams I remember in great detail, others are just fragments.

Because I had so many UFO/alien dreams, I sent Dr. Hynek only the most vivid, lucid memories.

Dream Log:

(1) I dreamt of a small silver disc that had landed on a small pad of smooth rock. It was only a 2-person ship, and I instinctively knew I was to go with the pilot. He was tall and wore a bland beige jumpsuit of some sort. Up we soared and quickly sped over the Earth. A long line of row houses faded fast and I realized that this was not the Earth I knew. We continued past the moon and beyond until I spied the giant mothership. It was like a city in the sky: massive and grey with many different smaller ships circling and entering… coming and going.

(2) I awoke from this dream pulling at my sleeves. I remember scrubbing my hands and arms. I was trying to get the green off. I had to get the green off or someone would discover that I'm an alien.

(3) I remember speaking in my dream: "More chocolate? How about some more spaghetti? I'm so happy you came," A group of tall Greys with big black eyes sat at my dining room table. Then I was following a human-looking alien to my craft. I recall being surprised at the sheer number of the spacecraft. They were of all sizes, shapes, and colors.

(4) There was blinding light, then total darkness. A strange noise outside my window startled me to full consciousness. Where had I been? What was I doing? I wasn't here a moment ago... I remember being someplace, but where? I recall flying through a closed door without splintering the wood or shattering the glass. Somehow we had changed the vibratory rate of the molecules and atoms that made up the door and flew right through it. I had looked back and the door was whole and undisturbed. Then it dawned on me that I was flying in a small UFO with two upright chairs. The pilot let me fly the small craft and I felt as though I had done this many times before. I call to mind sitting in front of the controls, feeling completely exhilarated as I moved swiftly through the clouds. I spied the huge mothership and I steered the craft toward it.

(5) I dreamt I was gliding up a staircase in the sky to a ship that was waiting for me. As I looked down, there were rows of identical townhomes. It was not Earth, at least not the Earth I recognized as home. I was delighted to be on the ship again.

(6) In one of the more uncanny dreams, I was in an operating room. My head was open and two alien doctors were saying they were going to "change my tapes." During the operation, they were shocked to learn that my "tapes" were permanent and could not be changed or updated. My life had been pre-programmed from the beginning to unfold in accordance with a specific plan and could not be tampered with or interrupted.

(7) I dreamt I was in a clinical facility aboard a spaceship. Reclining in something that was similar to a dentist chair with a metal cap over my skull, I felt a pulse of the machine being activated. Suddenly, my consciousness began to expand and I left my body. Flying through space, I could see heaven, which was more beautiful than words can describe. I kept saying, "Oh wow, oh wow." I didn't want to wake up.

(8) I overheard the aliens talking about a download. After they had left the room I felt drugged, as if I were paralyzed. Two assistants came in the room and took me by the underarms and dragged me out into the hall. I told them, "I want to see the man in charge!" They helped me up and again my legs were too weak to walk, so I was dragged down the hall to a double door to where the man in charge resided. The next thing I know, I'm in a bed in a recovery room.

(9) I watched a cold, robotic woman perform her duties of caring for the patients. I saw others in the room. Next to me was a woman on a bed with a man sitting in a chair by her side. The robotic woman said, "I don't know why they let you see the man in charge. No humans ever see him – only us."

(10) I could see many spacecraft in the sky – most were the smaller craft coming to pick up different people. One man came to my door. He was dressed in a military uniform and introduced himself as "UFO Jim." I knew I was supposed to go with him, so I followed him to his craft.

(11) With a foreboding feeling that a disaster was about to occur, I looked up into the heavens. The skies were filled with UFOs of all shapes: football, triangle, egg, saucer, rectangle, and cigar. Somehow I knew these ships were stationed to rescue as many people as possible and they had the capability to evacuate Earth's entire population in a matter of minutes.

UFO Shapes

(12) I was way out in space looking back at Earth. I was screaming inside my head, "It's lurching off its axis!" Overwhelmed with panic, I watched as the oceans sloshed up one side then down

again. The Earth looked like it was off kilter and wobbled like a toy top about to fall.

(13) I was standing beside a long line of people who were waiting to have blood drawn before embarking on a large mothership. My job was to assist and help calm people who were frightened.

(14) A craft, piloted by a humanoid alien, arrived for me. As we took off, the pilot talked about an alternate reality that has another Earth identical to ours. He told me we are on that other Earth also.

(15) From the craft's observation room, I looked deep into the inky darkness of space. Attached to my nose and mouth was a long white accordion-like tube that dangles down to my waist. The device helped me to breathe.

(16) From a small craft, I was directed to a mountain where there's a secret alien base. I couldn't see the entrance until the side of the mountain yawned and several spaceships escaped from the opening. I recognized the Havasupai Indian Reservation and its distinctive waterfalls – I knew I was in Northern Arizona. I remember looking down at the brownish green water of the Colorado River as I flew toward the secret base.

I actually welcomed the UFO dreams at this point and I looked forward to going to bed to dream again. I did not know what triggered these dreams until later.

(17) I was shown a planet whose residents followed their passion. Their work was not "work" to them and they loved their jobs. They labored for a short time each day on a project to benefit the entire community, and then devoted the rest of the day to develop whatever talent they possessed. Whether it was music, art, sports, gardening, or some sort of recreation to relax, it was theirs to pursue. They also put a lot of effort into interpersonal relationships. There was no war, no

greed, lust, or anger that I could see. The people cared deeply for one another and spoke the truth. They seemed to be very connected to the point that if one felt pain, it affected the entire group (and vice versa). The entire culture was in a state of joy the majority of the time.

(18) I dreamt I was taken aboard a craft for an extended stay. I ate something that looked like dried oatmeal. When I asked about it, I was told those flakes were dried earthworms. There were two aliens from Alpha Centauri who looked after me. They were perfect physical specimens of the human man and woman. We were among the stars in a large cargo vessel -- I was just along for the ride because I desired having the experience.

(19) I was with a group of people and we were dressed in night fatigues. It was dark, but the moon and stars provided a dim blue light. We were getting ready to repel down the side of a rocky cliff – it was part of the training. A bat wing-shaped UFO flew over Camelback Mountain in Phoenix ejecting pods. I can see people in the pods in suspended animation, floating in some kind of emulsion.

(20) I stood among the others watching the pods slowly fall from the sky. There was a nervous tension, because we knew we needed to get to them quickly so they could drink the "ice water potion" to wake up. It was explained to me that this is how our planet was seeded. This dream was so vivid that I later built a model using tinker toys of the spacecraft dropping the pods.

I was not frightened in any of these dreams. There was never any kind of element of panic or stress attached to any event, association, or communication with the other Beings. I was always happy to see the aliens.

(21) Three orbs of colored light arrived in my dream. All of the people around me were frightened of them. I was not. Knowing them

to be peaceful, I communicated with these glowing light Beings. They radiated a very high spiritual feeling of love and acceptance, and I knew they had come to help lift our level of consciousness. I felt nothing but love toward them.

(22) I dreamt of the Queen of Heaven who had arrived in a large silver disc. She was very beautiful and radiated love and peace.

(23) Four football-shaped UFOs flew from east to west above my home in Phoenix. There was an orange circular appendage with a cross dissecting the middle of the circle that was attached to the top of these craft. It reminded me of a radar appendage that tracked the weather.

(24) We were in caves underground, regrouping. There were stacks and stacks of supplies along the walls. We were waiting to go out, but it wasn't safe. I could see black helicopters hovering outside.

(25) I dreamt of a flying platform in the sky above tall pine trees in Northern Arizona. On this platform was a rectangular structure which reminded me of a mobile home, but it was some sort of space station. I resided in a house on the side of the mountain among the pines trees. My home served as a meeting place for those who had come from the stars.

(26) Again I dreamt of the mountain and the secret alien base – I watched the mountain slide open and eject a landing pad to accommodate my small craft. Then I was entering a dimly-lit conference room in the downstairs portion of my home. I flashed on all of the planning that had taken place here for the good of all mankind and planet Earth. I felt delighted to help facilitate these plans. A very tall, thin alien Ambassador entered the room wearing flowing robes and a dark triangular breastplate. He is at least 8 feet tall, and because we knew he'd be here, doorways and ceilings were elevated during the construction of the house. He was a loving entity, and I remember thinking how privileged I felt to be in his presence.

(27) In this dream, I stood at the edge of a meadow where a small craft on three legs sat on the ground. Small grey aliens moved

up and down a ramp going in and out of the craft. Several aliens were looking all around as if they had lost something – or they were very interested in something on the ground. They didn't realize that I was watching them. I had the feeling that I was in Oak Creek Canyon near West Fork between Sedona and Flagstaff.

Occasionally, I would dream of a Disney character mixed in with the aliens and UFOs. I've seen Cinderella's fairy godmother, the mice who change into white carriage horses, the Mad Hatter, and the Queen of Hearts from Alice in Wonderland. These familiar cartoon characters lent a "Fantasia"-like effect that is often associated with UFO experiences. (It is interesting to note that the Disney Studios artist who animated some of these characters, Ward Kimball, was also a student of UFOs and alien visitors.)

I also had many dreams that featured black helicopters – a phenomenon that is often reported in conjunction with UFO sightings. One time the helicopter in my dream was filled with milk, and an alien made a reference to the ancient Babylonian land of Sumer, which is also known as the land of "milk and honey."

At the time I created the dream log, I was a gyn/surgical nurse, so I was not surprised to have had multiple dreams about being a midwife. In these dreams, I am assisting in the birth and there are a lot of pregnancies. I was told that I had a job of great importance. Many of these dreams also left me with the impression that I was an integral part of the project to create a new hybrid race that was to populate the Earth.

Dis

In one dream, I learned that Las Vegas is a portal to other dimensions. In this dream, I was standing in front of an unusual window that peered into an alternate reality. I could see the "me" very clearly on the other side. Her name was Jane and she had shoulder-length brown hair. We simply looked and observed each other as the pilot told me about the Earth in the next dimension. He said we are there in that reality as well. I believe I had a glimpse of that other reality and of one of my other selves.

I was once shown an entrance to another dimension. I was told that I would know where and when this portal would be open so I could lead people through it to safety. I had the distinct feeling that the portal was near Airport Mesa in Sedona, Arizona.

I also experienced other lucid dreams of high strangeness that seemed somehow related to the UFO dreams:

(28) I thought I woke up but I was lying in bed completely paralyzed. I could only move my eyes. I surveyed the room. Next to the door were two gold coffins with mummies standing inside. The coffins moved and I watched them open and shut. Then I noticed that the ceiling was round like the inside of a ball, as were the walls, and covered in an Egyptian-motif fabric. I realized that I was not in my bedroom, but in a tomb... I had been buried alive! I was frightened, and the fear pulled me out of the vision. Suddenly, I was in my familiar bed again. I had the distinct feeling that I was an Initiate in an Egyptian Mystery School.

(29) I awoke to see a handsome bronze-colored man with a square chin and shining kind eyes stand over me. He wore a white short toga and sandals with straps up his legs. There was a gold cuff bracelet on his arm. A little boy stood next to him. As our eyes met, he screwed up his face into an odd little smile. The little boy's hair was brunette and very curly. I was just about to be shown a third person when I felt hands, real physical hands, reach under me. I was lifted off the bed. The realization of levitating above the mattress frightened me. I jerked myself back into full consciousness.

(30) I dreamt of Peru where I was watching llamas. The night sky seems incredibly close and filled with stars. Looking at one particular astrological configuration, the sky looked just like a stained glass window in a cathedral. I woke up knowing that I had just had a significant prophetic dream.

(31) I was underwater standing between tall columns on the *Greece* veranda of a Grecian-style building. I was holding a golden ball, and dressed in a draped Grecian-style gown. Three small saucer-shaped discs broke the calm surface above and descended rapidly. The discs passed by, heading for the nearby docking station.

(32) Standing in a Healing Temple, I was surrounded by huge crystals of vividly brilliant colors. There were pools of healing waters *crystals* here and there. It is serenely peaceful. This was where I lived.

There were also multiple dreams of calamities. Many were of tidal *Tidal* waves so high that no one could escape their onslaught. In a recurring *Waves* dream, the ground trembles, opening great big cavities all around me. Buildings were either flooded or on fire. Debris of all kinds crashed to the Earth while balls of fire rained down upon rich and poor alike. There were nuclear explosions, terrible winds, global famine, drought, pestilence, disease, tornadoes, hurricanes, volcanic eruptions, terrible pollution that brought death and terror. Many humans left their physical containers for newer, bright, and more promising incarnations. Others sought the safe harbors of alien ships or inner Earth. But the majority *Di* of mankind chose to leave for another dimension to begin anew.

These are just a sample of the strange UFO dreams I had experienced for a period of four years in the late 1970s. They inspired me to read stacks of magazines, books, and attend lectures and conferences to educate myself. I talked about these dreams with several people who were also interested in the Unidentified Flying Objects phenomenon.

Included with this dream log, was a cover letter to Dr. Hynek asking for his help. I needed answers, or some sort of explanation.

Chapter 3

ICUFOR, 1985

Dr. Hynek did not answer my letter nor did I hear what he thought of my dream log. I never heard if the dream log was forwarded to Hynek's colleague in Sweden. I did not receive any kind of correspondence from Dr. J. Allen Hynek, but never-the-less, our meeting was meant to be.

About five years after I sent the dream log to Dr. Hynek, I opened up Phoenix's daily newspaper, The Arizona Republic, only to read the headline, "Dr. J. Allen Hynek Brings UFO Research to Scottsdale."

It was a miracle! The article reported the opening of The International Center for UFO Research on Indian School Road. I considered the address and noticed that it was only a short drive from my home -- it was literally in my backyard. I thought this was kismet.

Monday, March 17th became the day I would go over to the ICUFOR address to meet the legendary Dr. J. Allen Hynek. I chose the date as personal power time because I was born on a Monday and on the 17th of the month.

After I completed my night shift at the hospital as a gyn surgical nurse, I went home, changed my clothes, got in the car, and drove over.

The International Center for UFO Research was not easy to find. It was located just off Indian School Road. There were just a few residential dwellings behind a glass and steel commercial building. The research center was within a small group of beige, angular-shaped townhouses.

When I got out of the car, a group of 7 to 10 people from all over were milling around on the front lawn. The front door stood open and people were walking in and out of the house, too. I stopped one of them and I asked, "Is this where Dr. Hynek lives?"

He looked to be a nice young man, wide-eyed and clean cut. He told me, "Well he's not here now... he's doing a TV interview downtown. Brian and Tina are with him." The young man looked right into my eyes as he spoke.

I didn't know who Brian and Tina were, but I thanked him and continued to move around with the others. I moseyed inside and got a look at the place. Obviously, someone was living there. It was a nice townhouse and it was furnished with the usual rented apartment furniture -- the walnut coffee table with the glass top, overstuffed everything, and like the exterior, everything was beige.

I met people from different places with a variety of experiences and talked to them. One young man had come all the way from California to discuss a sighting he had in the military with Dr. Hynek. Everyone had a story to tell. They were obviously people who followed UFOs and were aware of the latest research and sightings. I wrote a note to Brian and Tina saying I'd like to be involved in the project and would do whatever needed to be done. I left the note on the desk with my phone number.

A couple of days later I got a phone call from Brian Myers and volunteered my time to help set up the ICUFOR office in Scottsdale, Arizona. After working a full shift at the hospital, I'd go over and work 3 or 4 hours, to set up the office there. I also made up a form to fill out if anybody called with a sighting or an experience of any kind. I created office procedures and a filing system -- all of the basic clerical duties.

About 3 weeks later, I came face-to-face with Dr. J. Allen Hynek.

One Wednesday afternoon, as I was finishing up with a telephone call from someone reporting a sighting, Dr. Hynek walked into the office. Tina Choate and Brian Myers followed him, clinging to the man as if they were the static of freshly dried polyester. They had finagled an invitation to fly with Hynek to an official meeting later that day at Edwards Air Force Base in California and Brian and Tina wouldn't let Hynek out of their sight. There was to be something of interest for Dr. Hynek to see or hear about at the base. It was all very hush-hush, but there was much excitement on the part of Brian and Tina.

Hynek was smaller than I had envisioned him, with an "elfish" look about him. He had a slight build and stood no taller than five feet eight. His grey hair was whisked back neatly and his eyes seemed to twinkle behind thick horn-rimmed glasses. His snow-white mustache and goatee lent an impish look to his scholarly appearance of a professor. He wore a jacket with suede patches at the elbows and carried an unlit pipe.

As I shook Dr. Hynek's hand, I jogged his memory by saying: "You probably don't remember me, but I was the one that sent you a log of UFO dreams that I was having, and you had a colleague doing research..."

"Oh, yes, yes, yes... I remember" Of course, he did not remember me or my strange UFO dreams, he was just being polite. He told me he had sent the dream log onto his colleague, but had never gotten a return answer. It was a brief meeting.

As it turned out, Brian and Tina weren't allowed to attend the actual meeting at Edwards with Dr. Hynek. They flew with him out there, but Tina and Brian had to sit in a waiting room while Hynek was escorted to another part of the building or the base.

Dr. Hynek never shared with any of us what was discussed that day, so no one knew what happened there.

I hadn't been working very long for ICUFOR before Dr. J. Allen Hynek telephoned me. He said, "I have something to ask you... Would you be willing to come over and help set up my home office? I can't pay you much, only $100 a week. But if you could come and be my assistant..." His voice trailed off as if he were thinking about the moving van that was due to arrive at any time. "We're trying to get funding for this project and as soon as we get the funding, then I can pay you a regular salary."

What an opportunity! I said to myself. "Yes." I said to Hynek.

It was a lifetime chance to be right at ground zero in the UFO community that I couldn't pass up. I quit my job at the hospital and persuaded my mother to let me live rent-free in her townhouse for the six months I would be with Hynek.

As it turned out, my mother (who had a Unitarian/Universalist spiritual view) told me she had experienced a significant UFO dream herself. She was quite impressed with Hynek's credentials and was easily convinced that working for him was important to me and free rent was essential for me to survive economically. To make ends meet, I also had to supplement my income with a small savings account.

In the spring of 1985, I began working for Dr. J. Allen Hynek as his personal assistant. My duties included organizing his office and filing away copies of previously reported classified UFO cases reviewed and evaluated for the United States Air Force, including the many new accounts that flowed into our office.

Once the moving van arrived, I was kept busy setting up his office, while continuing my duties for ICUFOR of keeping records of UFO sightings and interviewing witnesses by phone.

As Hynek and I worked and got to know each other better, I discovered many things about him. For example, he was a typical absent-minded professor. He didn't care about filing or putting things away. He was very focused on the book he was working on at the time with Phillip Imbrogno called, "Night Siege." Hynek would have long conversations with Phillip on the phone.

Along one wall of his office ten large metal filing cabinets stood in a row. These were filled with case files Hynek had studied. The file cabinets were not locked.

In my spare time, I would often look through Hynek's UFO files, pull out a case and read it. Many of the official documents were a disappointment as there would be a title, date, and the rest was redacted. In one file, in the middle the lines of black ink blotting out the best information, was a list of the MJ-12 members.

At the time, "Operation Majestic Twelve" was a hot topic. A few months prior (December, 1984), the MJ-12 papers had been leaked to the press. The papers detailed the formation of the group in 1947 by an executive order from President Harry S. Truman called Majestic 12, or MJ-12. This was a secret committee of scientists, military leaders, and government officials who investigated UFO activity in the aftermath of the 1947 crash of an alien spaceship near Roswell, New Mexico. The document claimed that civilian and military witnesses were debriefed, and a cover story about weather balloons had been given to the press.

One live and four dead Beings, called "Extra-Terrestrial Biological Entities or EBEs," were recovered near the crash site. According to the documents, the military wanted more information about the recovered spacecraft and EBEs, how the craft worked, and the purpose for the alien visit. This led to the creation of Project Sign and Project Grudge. Although Hynek's name did not appear on the list of the Majestic 12 members, he acted as Science Advisor on both committees.

The list of prominent men that made up the MJ-12 group were connected to the highest levels of the military and national security. By the time the MJ-12 papers had become known in 1984, all of the members had passed away, so any questions for them will remain unanswered.

The members listed were: Sidney W. Souers (first Director of the CIA), Dr. Jerome Hunsaker (aircraft designer), Adm. Roscoe H. Hillenkoetter, (3rd Director of the CIA), Dr. Vannevar Bush (helped develop the nuclear bomb), Dr. Detlev Bronk (Atomic Energy Commission member), James V. Forrestal (Secretary of Defense, 1947), Gen. Hoyt S. Vandenberg (Director of Central Intelligence), Gen. Nathan F. Twining, (Commander, Wright-Patterson AFB), Gordon Gray (special assistant on national security to Pres. Truman), Lloyd V. Berkner (Joint Research and Development Board, 1946), Dr. Donald Menzel (Directory of Harvard College Observatory), and Gen. Robert Montegue (Commander, Sandia Atomic Energy Commission facility). I also recall seeing billionaire philanthropist, Laurence Rockefeller, mentioned in the Top Secret report.

Years later, I learned that Laurence Rockefeller had been pressing the Clinton administration (in office from 1993 to 2001) to open the government's UFO files. After Dr. Hynek passed away, I worked at the White House, and I was in attendance at Bill Clinton's birthday party. Unbeknownst to me at the time, while President Clinton was looking to receive re-election campaign funds, Mr. Rockefeller was looking for UFO disclosure.

The Rockefeller family, one of the world's wealthiest, had long been rumored to be the head of the global ruling elite. Active in international financial affairs, David Rockefeller is involved in the Trilateral Commission, the Council on Foreign Relations, and the Bilderberg Society. With all of the Rockefeller family members, it is often difficult to figure out where Rockefeller's business dealings end, and the shaping of multinational politics begins. It is not hard to believe that when a member of a family of this caliber wants the government to come clean on the subject of UFOs, it will happen.

Another story that I believed to be true was President Dwight D. Eisenhower's 1954 meeting with the extraterrestrials. While the president was on vacation in Palm Springs, he went missing to attend a top secret meeting with a representative of an alien species at the nearby Muroc Test Center, which is now called Edwards Air Force Base. This alien suggested that they could help us get rid of the Greys, but Eisenhower turned down their offer because they offered no technology. The cover story given to the press the next morning at a church service in Los Angeles explained that he had to have emergency dental treatment, according to former Naval Intelligence Officer and whistleblower, William Cooper.

As a member of the Intelligence Briefing Team for the Commander of the Pacific Fleet, Cooper had access to classified documents. Coming out with the "first contact" with Nordic ETs, Cooper wrote, "This alien group warned us against the aliens that were orbiting the equator and offered to help us with our spiritual development. They demanded that we dismantle and destroy our nuclear weapons as the major condition. They refused to exchange technology citing that we were spiritually unable to handle the technology which we then possessed. They believed that we would use any new technology to destroy each other. This race stated that we were on a path of self destruction and we must stop killing each other, stop polluting the Earth, stop raping the Earth's natural resources, and learn to live in harmony. These terms were met with extreme suspicion, especially the major condition of nuclear disarmament. It was believed that meeting that condition would leave us helpless in the face of an obvious alien threat. We also had nothing in history to help with the decision. Nuclear disarmament was not considered to be within the best interest of the United States. The overtures were rejected."

William Cooper also revealed that Eisenhower had a second meeting later in 1954 with ETs. This time, he met with a race of "Grey" aliens at Holloman Air Force base in New Mexico. Here, Eisenhower entered into a treaty with the aliens.

The treaty stated that the aliens would not interfere in our affairs and we would not interfere in theirs. If we would keep their presence on Earth a secret, they would furnish us with advanced technology and help us in our technological development. They could abduct humans on a limited and periodic basis for the purpose of medical examination and monitoring of our development, with the stipulation that the humans would not be harmed, would be returned to their point of abduction, and would have no memory of the event.

The aliens would also furnish MJ-12 with a list of all human contacts and abductees on a regularly scheduled basis. They also promised to not make any treaty with any other Earth nation.

By 1955, Eisenhower knew he had been deceived. The aliens had broken the treaty. Evidence had surfaced that the aliens were not submitting a complete list of human contacts, and not all abductees had been returned. There was very little if any advanced technology given in return. There was little the administration could do about the treaty that he had naively agreed to. Eisenhower had essentially surrendered because the aliens knew that what we most feared was disclosure.

The question of disclosure has long been debated. There is quite a dilemma about what would happen if UFOs were no longer secret. How would the populace react? Most of the Greys are friendly, however, we must ask if the US Military would face repercussions from the untrustworthy aliens in the event of full disclosure?

Although Dr. Hynek was very "closed-mouthed," and disclosed very little associated with his research and UFO knowledge, it was general knowledge within the ICUFOR center that the government continues to be involved in the UFO cover-up. There is just too much circumstantial and testimonial evidence in the UFO case files to support this idea.

If the Government does not disclose the truth, the ETs will show themselves. Disclosure is very important to me. For the past 30 years, I have told everyone who would listen about the ET presence. In recent years there has been a huge influx in sightings and the majority of Americans believe that we aren't alone in the universe.

Mark my words: the aliens will make themselves known soon -- while there is still time.

Chapter 4

The Conference and the Cosmic Experience

Dr. Hynek felt comfortable enough with my background and knowledge to ask me to represent him at the Conference for UFO Investigators and Contactees at the University of Wyoming in Laramie, July 11 through the 15th, 1985. The conference was organized by Dr. Leo Sprinkle, author of "Soul Samples," and Professor Emeritus at the University of Wyoming. Dr. Leo Sprinkle is well known for being one of the first academic scholars to investigate alien abduction, cattle mutilations, and UFO experiences.

Connie and Doug Tipton – two people who were active in the local UFO group there – helped Dr. Sprinkle organize the conference. (As a smoker, I met Doug on the porch outside the main conference room, but I didn't get a chance to meet Connie.)

I met a number of unusual people there. One gal from Japan, who was a member of the Raelian Movement, thought she was a robot plugged into an underground computer source where she gets all her information, a story rather like the story line in the 1999 movie, "The Matrix." She reported to have had two recent meetings with contactee Billy Meier about her story. Then she quizzed me about ICUFOR and the UFO activity in Arizona.

Keith McDonald, who was in regular contact with extraterrestrials from the planet Landa, and Ron Owen, were in attendance at the conference. They told me about their personal visions and alien messages of Earth's "metamorphosis." Keith considered this his "life work."

I also spoke with Jim Frazier and Brian Scott, who told me a similar story with respect to the "new" mankind. Brian Scott had presented evidence to President Jimmy Carter about the transformation of the common man. They warned him that it was going to take place on the planet whether the government recognized it or not -- in fact, we are now in this new age. Brian told the president, "Common man is changing right now and the new age accelerates the transformation in the near future."

WYO   A powerful energy vortex exists just outside Laramie where the Earth's ley lines cross. Considered a Native American "holy land," stories of the land's mystic powers go back hundreds of years. The bulk of the attendees had already made plans to visit "the ranch" by lunchtime on the first day of the conference.

The few who had already gone out there reported phenomena ranging from sights of crafts, aliens on the ground, strange animals and sounds, light flashes, portals opening and closing and close encounters with alien Beings. Even past visitors told strange and wonderful stories of this nature.

The owner of the ranch, Pat McGuire, wrote that back in the early 1970s, he was contacted by ETs who told him where to drill a well. Others had tried many times to drill for water on the land, including large corporate farms, but they were unsuccessful. The well the ETs guided Pat to supplied enough water for the entire area.

I repeatedly missed the groups going out to visit the ranch for one reason or another, even though I desperately wanted to go. Keith shared a story of an out-of-the-ordinary alien contact (even for our group). I ached to have my own experience even more after Keith McDonald told me it was one of the most significant experiences of his life. I was adamant that I'd see the ranch before returning home.

It was the end of the conference, with only the banquet dinner and ceremonial goodbye speeches remaining, when Doug sat down beside me.

"I understand you want to go out to the Ranch," Doug said. "When do you have to leave to go home?"

Considering the lateness of the hour, I had given up on being able to get out to the ranch. Doug Tipton offered a ride out to the ranch the following afternoon, so I decided to stay one more day.

That was Saturday, July 15th, 1985, and the final day of the conference. Up until that time, I hadn't met Connie. As the associate organizer for the conference, she was busy with her duties. I got glimpses of her throughout the day talking to the different speakers and attendees, but I did not get to know her.

I was just about to join Jerome Clark at the microphone for our remarks when I saw Keith McDonald. "I just spent a long time with Connie." He was quite animated and full of energy.

"Oh? Was it interesting?" I asked him. "What was it about?"

"Don't you know Connie?" he asked. He seemed surprised and somewhat amused.

"No, I don't know Connie." I said. "We've never met."

Keith leaned forward and whispered, "Oh, she's very, very special."

Keith's words proved true the following day when I visited the ranch. Connie was largely responsible for the soon-to-come dramatic physical contact I had with benevolent extraterrestrials.

I opened with "You're not crazy." I saw smiles and nodding heads in the audience. "The government knows about the worldwide sightings. They know and they are aware of the contacts and abductions."

Jerome Clark turned and eyed me suspiciously. I continued.

"The government knows more than you can possibly imagine. The whole government-military complex is in cahoots with the aliens and collaborating on many levels with many experiments."

Jerome Clark cleared his throat.

The audience gave me a standing ovation.

After Saturday night's closing banquet dinner, I joined a few other conference attendees at the local diner for "midnight coffee."

Connie, Doug, Jim Frazier, and I sat in a large booth in the back of the café and chatted until 3 in the morning. We had a lively discussion of Jim's video production of the "new man" transformation, Doug's philosophies learned from his contact with the ETs, and UFO experiences in general. I told them about my UFO dreams and my desire for contact and full disclosure.

As we parted, Doug reminded me that he planned to drive me to the ranch after my appointment with Dr. Sprinkle. We agreed to meet mid-afternoon.

When I got back to my room, I looked out to the brilliant and expansive night sky. In the high altitude and light pollution-free mountains of Wyoming, I felt as if I could see into the depths of space. I spied a particularly big star and spoke to it.

I said, "Here I am, all the way from Phoenix, Arizona. There's no reason why we can't have contact right here and now."

Suddenly, the arm my chin rested on started to disintegrate. I decided to lie down before I disappeared altogether. The whole room became less "essential," as my body vibrated from the top of my head to the tip of my toes.

I thought, "Well, I'm about to either levitate, have an out-of-body experience, or I'm going to be beamed up to that UFO." I laid my head on the pillow. My body vibrated deep in my being.

I closed my eyes and I could see it – a spaceship. It was round, donut-shaped, black with long windows. As I studied it, I noticed three or four people on the ground around the tire-shaped craft, and then I caught the movement of people inside.

The scene quickly shifted to a vision of a long Native American headdress made of illuminated gold feathers, with symbols embroidered on the headband in primary colors. I was at ritual… an ancient ceremony among many who were gathered there. The three priests dressed in garb that reminded me of Hawaii, held thick wooden staffs with plumes of vibrant colored feathers that whirled at the top as they danced.

At 5 a.m. the vision had faded and I realized that I had not slept. I made sleep a priority, because Sunday, July 16th, was to be a cosmic experience. I intuitively knew that what had just transpired was but a small morsel of what was to come.

On Sunday, the University of Wyoming campus was eerily quiet after all the excitement and energy surrounding the conference. I caught up with Dr. Leo Sprinkle at his study where he invited me to be part of his "psychic impressions" research project. As a therapist, Dr. Sprinkle was conducting hypnotic regression with UFO contactees. His ground breaking research set the standard for UFO research of "highly strange" experiences.

It was a little awkward at first because I had not talked with Sprinkle much during the conference. Although we knew little about each other, he quickly put me at ease. I soon fell into a relaxed state, as if I were floating in warm water in a quiet tropical lagoon. I felt safe.

Leo then psychically merged his being with mine and tapped into my soul. This "soul reading" left me with a fresh view – in spite of it being a gut-wrenching experience. I heard my words in Leo's voice, spewing the forgotten and ignored information I had held at the soul-level.

Leo brought me through eight of my past-life cycles, each with relevance to my life today. He explained the qualities and attributes I had brought forward into this life that would benefit me, the things that hindered my success, and other short-comings in my current life. It was as if he was having a running conversation with me, and yet I did not speak out loud. In the end, I had been given a gift of a "soul cleansing," and a glimpse of my true higher-self.

During the session, I felt myself morph into a bird of prey. I was looking out my stealth-like eyes, focusing, closing up my eyelids like an aperture of a camera. I knew I was the bird, and yet I felt captured -- imprisoned by someone or something -- as if I knew what it was like to be the Birdman of Alcatraz. I also felt the presence of a variety of entities, many dissimilar environments, and dimensional realms illuminated by prisms of exotic-colored light.

During the session, Dr. Leo Sprinkle zeroed in on a past life I had with Dr. J. Allen Hynek which directly affected my current life. Our past came together a long time ago – late 1400s or early 1500s – when Hynek was an astronomer and I was his assistant. (I immediately thought of how strange it is that life repeats itself!) In that life, Allen saw extraterrestrial spacecraft through his telescope and let me see them, too. However, he would not tell anyone about them and swore me to secrecy. I recalled being terribly frustrated about having to keep quiet about this other-worldly discovery.

In comparing my previous life to my current situation, it's as if the same thing has happened all over again. Hynek was always very cautious when speaking publicly on the subject of UFOs and never divulged everything he knew. Like my previous life, the lack of disclosure is frustrating and so I feel compelled to tell the world what I know about UFO occupants.

Unbeknownst to Leo, there had been a little cosmic war going on inside of me for some time. In my current life, the government cover-up of UFOs and their involvement with the extraterrestrials caused me to feel compassion for how poorly the contactees have been treated. The whole situation has been badly handled from a spiritual perspective, and "The Powers That Be" suppressed the common man with ridicule and shame.

A mismatched-looking alien came into sight: grey in color, its head larger than an ordinary human, with divergent features that somehow took on the appearance of a praying mantis. The arms had little thickness or depth. I watched as the bony hands and fingers reached out to me. The being's long weak-looking legs and feet reminded me of Mr. Peanut. It startled me how it resembled a humanoid and an insect at the same time.

alien

Our eyes met, and I felt a vibration on the top of my head – the same vibration I knew as a signal that my spirit guide was afoot.

I told Leo excitedly, "That's the being who taps me on the top of my head!" A mystery that had vexed me since the curious UFO dreams began was solved. I felt as if this being was the inspiration to the nightly dreams I had for four years about UFOs and other strange visions.

All the things that bound me fell away, and for once, I was totally relaxed. Leo asked me to go further into my subconscious.

I was standing in front of a massive, heavy door that was guarded on each side by a robot. The robot on the left was black and the one on the right was red. Telepathically, I received the message, "No admittance!" The session ended abruptly.

I truly enjoyed my time with Dr. Sprinkle and gave him high praise in the research reports feedback. I wrote "A plus to Dr. Leo Sprinkle --- who helped me attain a spiritual high. It was bliss."

"Praying Mantis Alien"

Following the soul-cleansing session with Leo, Doug and Connie took me to the ranch. I was still in a heightened state of psychic consciousness from Leo's session.

We piled into the truck's cab. When we crossed over the entrance of the property, I felt an up-rush of energy that made me dizzy.

Connie and Doug smiled when they saw my face.

"Did you feel that?" They nodded.

Of course, they were ready for it, having been at the ranch many times before. They were silently pleased that I was sensitive enough to feel what many miss.

Driving into the ranch, we caught sight of four antelope, which I learned later to be Connie's "sign" that it was OK to be on the property. Later, a whole herd of antelope appeared, which had spiritual meaning for all of us.

Doug stopped the truck at a wide clearing with scattered scrub brush growing out of rocky turf, among green tuffs of wildflowers with spent blooms.

"It seems to be necessary that you get out of the truck and walk the land," Connie said to me, "That seems to be some sort of rule."

I took off by myself, and headed toward a small rise amongst rolling hills. Here I found cement garden statues of Jesus and Mary. These marked a baby's small grave. I prayed for the child, and for myself.

I asked my Master, Maharaji, to please let me have an encounter or contact with highly benevolent Beings. I meditated while looking at the endless view. Just below where I stood was a large flat area, etched with three distinct rings. I also noticed a mountain that looked like a pyramid, and a depression in the Earth between two hills that sites another mountain range.

Doug explained that the formation was called "the window," and was reported to be a spot where the ley lines and Earth energies are optimum for spaceships to enter our dimension. Ley lines are magnetic lines that birds, animals, and other life forms use to migrate across long distances. Structures such as Stonehenge, ancient temples and cathedrals or highly spiritual areas such as Sedona, Arizona or the Giza Plateau in Egypt, are often found along these lines. Where they intersect, a cosmic vortex is created and Earth's natural energy is very high. These areas are often considered to be sacred.

At first, I was a little shy to admit my nervousness in the extraordinary experience I intuitively knew was about to occur. I still knew nothing of Connie and Doug Tipton, but I remained open to whatever was happening.

I began walking the land. I was not ready for a hike – I wore uncomfortable shoes amongst brush, rock, and uneven terrain. The sun was dim behind a partly-cloudy sky and I had no jacket.

A couple of people from another car started to follow me, but Connie stopped them saying, "No, this is Ann's turn. Let her be alone." We parted company.

I spied the same herd of antelope beneath the "window" area. They began to stir, charge, then stampede as if they had been spooked. Connie and Doug came up and we all watched in amazement. "That means a ship has come through the window," Connie said, "and it frightened the antelope."

I didn't see anything... but what followed next defies current understanding or logic.

Two big buck antelope came close and stood like sentries next to a large pile of standing stones and looked me right in the eye. As soon as I "got" the message that I was to stand next to the rock pile, the bucks ran off. I whispered a mantra, a prayer of protection, and a request that contact, should it happen, be enlightening.

After a moment, I walked over to where Connie was watching the antelope through binoculars. Doug squatted and scratched the dirt with a stick producing the image of three spaceships.

"These are the shapes of the ships that I'm picking up and there seem to be four of them, one large, and three small. They're directly behind the sun." He wiggled his fingers in the air, and received some sort of communication. I tried to do the same, but again, nothing.

Suddenly, something made me close my eyes. An image of a star map appeared on the inside of my eyelids. Light streaked across from star to star, details became refined and I saw an area of the sky with a circle around it.

Star Map

Doug got the same impression at the same time, and was able to distinguish a few more details. It was a star map not unlike the map reported by Betty Hill in her abduction story. I felt a tap on my head and perceived the insect-being's presence once again, and got the impression that he had come in one of the invisible spacecrafts Doug drew a picture of in the dirt.

The cold wind picked up. I stepped behind the rock pile where it was a little warmer out of the icy breeze. Doug and Connie stood nearby.

I closed my eyes and said, "There's a woman here and she has a wreath of flowers around her head. Her hair is long. There's also a man with her."

"I have the impression that they have to ask permission," Doug offered.

Immediately, I felt the presence of my master, Maharaji in my third eye, giving me permission. Instinctively, I put my arms out while keeping my eyes closed and became aware of a physical sensation -- a powerful vibration as though a beam of light pierced the center of my forehead and then radiated throughout my body. It seemed Doug and Connie were miles away, and I was being lifted up and bathed in an overpowering pink light.

I could feel the pulse of infinite energy. The pink light burned hot to a brilliant white. An intense heat filled my body and I got the sense of someone jamming a steel rod down the back of my head, down my spine, and out my tailbone. I felt pain, the white light, the fierce energy of it all, vibrating like an emotional sensation through my whole being.

The energy coursed from the top of my head, down my spine, completely through me and out my left leg. I began to cramp, and willed myself to breathe through the pain. I said to myself, "It's OK, you can stand it, you can stand it, whatever it is, it's good, it's happening to you, it's all good…"

I grabbed the back of my neck to staunch the pain running up into my head. My body shook vigorously. Unsteady, I collapsed to my knees. A ball of light exploded inside my head, a physical quality like 4th of July sparklers going off inside my head ensued. The episode ended when I fell forward to take the weight off my left leg, giving sway to the ardent pounding at the base of my skull.

Two powerful thought forms that went through my mind at the time were: "I am going somewhere," and "We are changing souls." It was an extra-dimensional event that was so complex that I cannot begin to understand it. From that moment on, I have felt as if I knew what it was like to be an alien in human form; I experienced a moment of high clarity when I knew I was one with the universe, a Starseed.

Connie and Doug appeared and asked if I was all right. I told them that I didn't think I could stand due to the cramp in my leg. Connie began to rub my leg as I sat and rested. I started telling her what had happened when she called Doug over.

"Look at her eyes, Doug." I looked at Doug so he could look at me. "Her blue eyes are bleached completely white."

I explained what had happened and fully expected that they would take me home. My thinking was muddled from the kundalini-like experience. But I was feeling stronger, so we kept walking, watching our feet as we moved across the land.

We found a rock whose markings looked like a hand and a skinny, thin arm that looked like the hand and arm of the insect being that tapped my head. An ancient wrinkled face stared up at me on another stone.

I moved toward the flat lands below. My stomach growled from hunger and the wind whipped my chilly, bare arms. I suggested that we return to the campus for food and warmer clothes.

Connie closed her eyes and signaled for quiet. She announced, "It's OK. They'll wait for us to return."

We returned to the truck at sunset when the sky was ablaze with colors. The other people who came along were waiting, and each had had their own experiences. As we were leaving the property, lightening danced across the sky with an intensity that I had never experienced before. We remarked on the dark faces formed by the clouds, and how the electric arrows flickered and pierced the approaching black sky of fading light.

We hadn't gone far when the truck ran out of gas.

Connie and Doug had owned their truck for several years and had never run out of gas. It was as if it were a ruse to make sure we stayed at the ranch to watch the incredible lightening show that continued overhead. Dark, threatening clouds approached as lavender-edged flashes of jagged light reached down to a sky colored brilliant orange from the dying light of day. I couldn't tear my eyes away.

While Doug dashed off to the nearest farm to fetch the petrol, I chatted absent-mindedly to the others about the lightening storm. All agreed that we had never seen lightening like this before.

Once again, my eyelids spontaneously closed and I saw visions of something very real in the most fundamental sense of the word. Besides the star map, I was "shown" five symbols: an emerald-cut crystal or diamond illuminated by white light, a Maltese cross, an arrow pointing up, a trident with a 5-pointed star, and a dragon in the sky.

Doug soon returned with the gas and we headed back to town in pouring rain a little after 10 pm – I thought it was earlier because the sun had just set. When I told Dr. Hynek about this later, he suggested that I had a period of missing time.

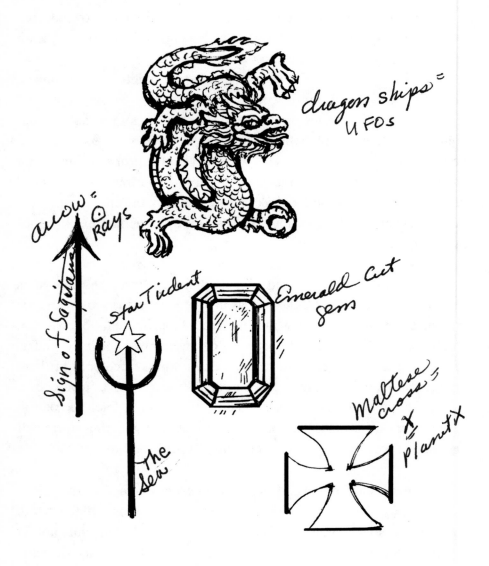

"Five Symbols"

Dr. Hynek did not attend the conference because he was too busy researching and writing for "Night Siege" with Philip Imbrogno. The tome is considered a classic in UFO in-depth investigation of high strangeness in New York's Hudson Valley. Hynek discovered that missing and distorted time was common during contact or sightings, so it made sense that he would mention it.

When the group arrived back into town it was 10:30 pm and I had the feeling that it took longer to return than to drive out to the ranch. I left Dr. Sprinkle's office at 3:45 pm and went to the center. We left the center shortly after I arrived and drove out to the ranch, arriving there about 5 pm. After the intense experience, we gathered at the truck to watch the sun go down. Doug returned with gas rather quickly, and yet it was very late -- 10:30 pm -- when we arrived at the only restaurant still open in town.

We enjoyed lighthearted conversation over dinner, although I was completely wound up by the profound adventure. It wasn't long before the topic turned to the vision of the five symbols. These token symbols came to me as we returned from the ranch. Riding in the back of Doug's truck, I would close my eyes, only to see an allegorical three-dimensional picture.

When I explained how I saw the dragon whipping its tail across the sky, the Japanese student, Akiko Arakawa, told us a story. A familiar legend in Japan tells of a Dragon in the Sky that becomes a spaceship. The people run out to greet the alien pilots, and they are told that no harm will come to them. The aliens are treated reverently as people feel blessed to be around them. Then all the people get together to prepare a feast to celebrate their presence before they depart. They promise to come back and people are told to look for the Dragon in the sky.

As she spoke, my third eye opened and I could see the UFO landing in my mind. I wondered out loud if this symbol confirms my belief that UFOs will soon land in public view. I also thought it was a good omen.

Akiko's story also reminded me that a "Dragon in the Sky" is a common historical name for UFOs. Even today, the Solomon Islanders share sightings of the "dragons" that fly in and around the islands.

However, my first impression of this image was that it looked like a planet that from Earth had the appearance of a fiery dragon. In

January 1983, the New York Times reported, "something out there beyond the farthest reaches of the known solar system seems to be tugging at Uranus and Neptune. Some gravitational force is perturbing the two massive planets, causing irregularities in their orbits."

I immediately thought that the image of the Dragon in the Sky, flipping its red fiery tail, was none other than Planet X, also known as the 12th planet, or Nibiru. It is currently in front of the sun, but it won't be long before it's visible to everyone on Earth.

The vision of the dragon was followed by an upright trident with a five-pointed star on the top of the middle (shorter) prong. Since tridents are commonly associated with Poseidon/Neptune, the god of oceans and seas, I thought of water and its quiet strength.

Since then, I have learned that there have been trident and star crop circles in England that have been proven to be strangely associated with the Mayan calendar, counting down the days before the Mayan calendar ends. At the World Trade Center Memorial Plaza, two tridents stand sentry at the front door. These were made from the melted aluminum studs and formed into tridents after the tragedy of 9/11, and now are received as the iconic stars in the museum pavilion.

The sense of drama and sadness I had as the symbol struck my vision might have been a warning of what still is to come.

The symbol that perplexes me most is that of the emerald-cut gem. The afternoon was cloudy, but the clouds, dark and heavy with rain, did not move, although I noticed something that looked like it was moving behind the clouds. I closed my eyes, and using third-eye vision, I watched an object appear.

The object was elongated and dark around the edges, but it sparkled like a diamond. It was gem cut with facets across the top and down the length of it, reminding me of an emerald, yet giving off a pure white, crystal-clear illumination.

By the time I began to really concentrate on the chisel-edged object, it vanished and I was soon shown a Maltese cross. The cross of course, is an "X" -- as in "Planet X." As I explained to Connie, this symbol reminded me of the Knights Templar. Dr. Hynek had a large formal portrait of himself hanging in his living room where he is wearing a dark ring with a gold and white Maltese cross. This led me to believe that this experience was somehow tied to my employment with Dr. Hynek.

The final symbol was a solid arrow pointing straight up. Throughout history, the arrow has symbolized war, power, swiftness, rays of the sun, knowledge, as well as deities. Apollo and goddess Artemis (both hunters), the Hindu weather god, Rudra; and various gods of sexual attraction such as Eros (Greek), Cupid (Roman), Kama (Hindu) are represented by arrows. Native Americans drew or painted "sacred medicine arrows" on objects as symbols of power.

At first, I thought the arrow was simply pointing up, as in "we're up here if you'd care to look." A rune featuring an arrow is a symbol for a spiritual warrior, and I certainly feel like I'm fighting the good fight getting this message out. I also thought of the message, "Come up, come up" I received during an automatic writing session years before. Connie and Doug agreed with these simple explanations.

By the time we finished our meal, and with every nuance of the symbols I had envisioned thoroughly scrutinized, Connie stood up. "I think we're onto something here. We've got to go back to the ranch."

I agreed.

Although my intentions were good, my energy ran out. With a full stomach, warmer clothes, and the lateness of the hour, returning to the ranch just then was as big a task as climbing Mt. Fuji after running a marathon. At the same time, I did not want the day to end. I had the uncanny feeling that I would continue to receive messages with a higher consciousness, and this communication would continue until the rain stopped. Somehow, it was extremely important for the three of us to be in the same room in the hours ahead.

"Connie?" I asked, "Why don't you guys just bring your blankets and pillows from the truck and stay here tonight?" The dorm was vacant, except Akiko, who was staying another night, and the dorm "parents," who knew Connie and Doug very well since they all worked for the university.

I grabbed three large coffees, Doug and Connie grabbed their gear, and we headed up to my dorm room. We put two mattresses together on the floor for Doug and Connie's bed and made ourselves comfortable. While Doug went to take a shower, Connie and I got to know each other.

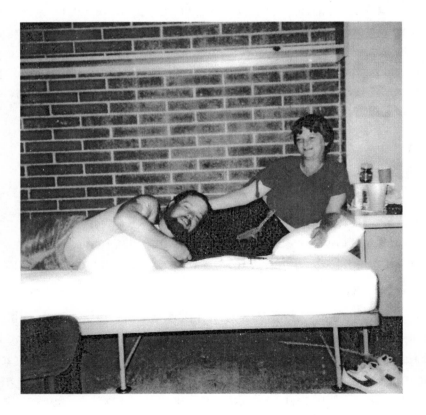

"Connie and Doug Tipton on bed in dorm"

She told me a little about their experiences with UFOs and how they have been following a spiritual quest for communication with higher consciousness Beings. Doug returned and we continued to share stories. We talked about the books we had read, current events, and "Alternative Three."

All three of us were familiar with the story: in 1977, Science Report, a television show in England known for its factual research and scientific approach, broadcast a documentary about secret bases on the moon and Mars, PSYOPS operations, Earth changes and the New World Order. Alternative Three, or ALT3, explains that the Illuminati enrolled a panel of scientific experts to determine if the world was actually headed for disaster, and if so, what could they do about it? The group came up with three alternatives: as written in the book by Leslie Watkins with David Ambrose and Christopher Miles.

1. Blast "chimneys" in the stratosphere with nuclear weapons releasing heat and pollution. Project status abandoned.

2. Relocate Earth's population in massive underground caverns drawing fresh, cool air from the soil. Project status abandoned.

3. A bold venture into space built on revolutionary technology, officially sanctioned murder, and a secret international conspiracy. Project status unknown.

However, in the book *Alternative Three* by Ken Mitchell these original alternatives had taken on a different even more sinister tone. He describes the three as:

* Alternative 1—to drastically reduce the human population on Earth.

* Alternative 2—to construct vast underground shelters to house government officials until the crisis had stabilized;

* and Alternative 3—to establish a "Noah's Ark" colony of humanity's best and brightest off of the planet, preferably on Mars.

After the Alt3 conversation, I was so tired that I reclined on my bed and put my head on my hand. Connie mentioned that it was 3:10 in the morning, and even though I thought the long day was ending, there was still more to come.

3+6 AM   "You do realize that the hours between 3 am and 6 am are called 'angel hours,' don't you?" Connie asked me. She said that these three hours are when the spiritual energies are closer to the world. (This is the same reason that I was taught to meditate between these hours.)

As I watched Connie speak, it appeared as if her face changed. I sat up and took notice. Connie did not look like Connie at all – her face had definitely become different. She looked like a different person! Then, her face changed again, and again. One face replaced the next flickering like a fast-paced slide show.

"Unbelievable," I said under my breath. I noticed that Doug wasn't watching Connie's face contort into different people. "Connie! Your face…it's changing!"

Doug stopped talking. The air in the room was electric. Sounds dissipated.

Connie held out her hand. "Take my hand, Doug. This is going to be a heavy one!"

*"Alien Females and Higher Power
(The Sisterhood of Light)"*

I was unsure of what Connie meant and I didn't know quite what to expect.

Connie was a small woman with a pixie-face, round with an angular chin, short curly brown hair, large golden eyes that sparkled when she smiled. But as she sat across from me holding onto Doug's hand, I watched in amazement as her cheekbones grew higher, her cheeks looked hollow, and her forehead grew wider and longer, while her nose all but disappeared.

Another woman's face, neck and shoulders, was coming through and on top of Connie. The face changed several times, and each time, it was a different female. Connie said later that she had her eyes closed through the whole thing. I was unaware of that because these big eyes were wide open and looking right at me.

At last, one of them spoke:

"You desired to see us in the physical," she said to me, "we hope this will appease you." Neither the voice nor the vocabulary sounded like Connie, yet under the face like a translucent mask, I could see Connie's lips move.

I could hardly wrap my head around what was happening.

I studied this person sitting in front of me -- her face was wide, and her eyes were definitely larger than normal, the shape of her face was angular, with a pointed chin and small thin lips that looked like a crescent moon when she smiled. She was wearing some kind of headdress. Her gaze was magnetic.

Then, like a kaleidoscope changing patterns, many "Extra-Celestial" Beings came in and shared Connie's body. The room was crowded with these Beings. It felt as if I were in the most sacred cathedral in a room full of saints and angels. They were all female.

During the hour that followed, these Beings came through and projected love in such abundance and quality that my heart melted. Their compassion brought tears to my eyes and I could not stop them from streaming down my face. I couldn't believe that they had actually come and had chosen this vehicle by which to show themselves to me.

One woman came in and put her left hand up as in a greeting. I mimicked her hand signal and so did Doug. When she left, another came in.

She said, "You may now ask your questions."

I was unprepared and tongue-tied. I thanked them for coming and showing themselves and their love to me. I finally thought to ask, "Where are you from?"

The moment I asked, two words popped into my mind. There was a word, and then the abbreviation for that word. For example, we say "Los Angeles" or "L.A." for short. I understood both the long and short form of the word at the time, but it seems to have been immediately erased from my memory. But I know that these Beings were inter-dimensional and also extraterrestrial. I had the distinct feeling that I almost could remember them. They appeared as "Sisters" to me, however the Higher Power Being was most definitely my "teacher." I also had the feeling that I was part of a sisterhood.

I later called these Beings the "Sisterhood of Light."

"Is my mission on target?" I asked, "Will it be accomplished?"

Again, I felt their grace, "Yes, the mission would be completed."

What the mission is, I don't know, but it seemed as if I knew exactly what they were talking about at the time. It seemed like a reasonable question to ask. I was left with the impression that I had work to do.

"Are my dreams prophetic?"

Again, I received an affirmative answer anchored in loving thoughts.

After answering a few personal questions from Doug, the benevolent Being said, "We will now yield to a higher power."

Connie's face and demeanor changed again. This new channeled Being seemed much older. I noticed a lot of wrinkles and the face was ancient with wisdom. The neck elongated and there seemed to be folds of skin, as if there were too much skin for the frame, making her look similar to the ET character in the ET movie. Or rather more like the entity that disembarked from the mothership at the conclusion of Close Encounters of the Third Kind. This Great Being was all love and wisdom. Her eyes were large and incredibly beautiful. I wanted to embrace her with my whole heart.

My back straightened. It was hard to imagine talking to a higher power – this Being exuded calm, serenity, and love.

I asked, "What happened to me out at the ranch today?"

"In your language, you would call it an initiation to a higher level," she told me. "You've been given higher or greater powers and you will now be receiving communications directly."

This was stunning news. I was happy and apprehensive at the same time. Before I could ask how I would receive these communications directly I could see Connie's face contort once again.

One of the lesser females had an upswept ornament in her hair, which held three pheasant looking feathers. It caught my attention because it set her apart from the others and the fact that she popped in and out about 3 times. I remarked about her appearance later to Doug and he confirmed what I had seen. "Yes, he said, "the ornament kind of swooped across her head."

Doug asked, "Would Ann be working with me and Connie?"

"Not before you form what you would call a triangle with the Being that was known to this channel 22 years ago. When she remembers who that being is, you, Doug, will also remember."

This answer puzzled me and I did not receive any further information.

"Will you stay with me?" I wanted to know if I would always feel their guidance.

They answered, "We have always been with you," and I suppose they told me something I already knew at the soul level.

"When may I join you?"

"When the time is appropriate," came my reply.

"We must withdraw quickly so this channel can breathe."

The Beings withdrew to the ethers, and Connie morphed back into herself once again. Her eyes were closed as she struggled for a deep breath. She gasped as she fell over onto the mattress.

"Connie!" I jumped up thinking she was dead.

Her breathing was steady, and her pulse slowed to a normal rate. As she came out of the trance, she opened her eyes slowly, blinked, and smiled. Doug propped her up in his arms.

"May I have a drink of water?" Her voice was weak; she barely spoke above a whisper.

After a few minutes, Connie seemed her normal self. We talked excitedly, replaying every moment and every question so nothing would be forgotten.

Connie said that it was the most intense channeling she had ever done. She didn't know how many Beings actually came through, but she was very aware of the changes she felt by their presence. She could feel her body change from the solar plexus up. From the waist down, she remained the same.

When the higher power Being took over her body, she was completely taken out with no awareness or memories of what happened. She had lost consciousness altogether at that point.

"Connie," I said, "I had no idea that you were a trance medium."

"It is strange, Ann. This has only happened to me once before – and for a very brief time. I received a message for a friend." Connie looked as blown away as I felt. "I had no idea what was going to happen, but there was so much power, well, that's why I asked Doug to hold my hand."

We relaxed and remained in quiet reflection for a few minutes when Connie bolted upright.

"They're coming back," Connie's eyes were again growing large. "Doug, quick! Take my hand."

Something brushed against my arm. Doug grabbed her hand with one hand, and supported her back with the other.

Connie's voice changed pitch, "This is to be a training session for Ann to recognize the tap on the head and the ringing in the ears as a time to open her channel."

I was instructed that when I felt the Being's presence it would feel like a tap on the head and there would be a ringing in my ears. In this practice session, I was further instructed to concentrate on Doug when I felt this. Doug was to concentrate on me and we were to bring our "vibration" in tune with each other.

"There will be four rapid transmissions," the wise one told me, "You must reach out and take Doug's hand."

Doug reluctantly took his hand off of Connie's back and held it out.

I felt the vibration on the top of my head, and the ringing in my ears, but I was at a loss on how to "open my channel." I took a deep, relaxing breath and calmed my mind, while closing my eyes and visualizing Doug's energy.

I received nothing. I didn't see or hear any words or symbols, I heard no music; the only thing I felt at the moment was that I felt tired.

The lesson continued, "We will go now so you can remember what has transpired." With that, the Being was gone and Connie returned to consciousness.

"That was a bust for me," I said, disappointed, "I didn't get a thing."

Doug patted my hand, "Well, I did." He reported four very definite sensory feelings: a rapid heartbeat, a cramping in the solar plexus, his hair on the back of his neck stood on end, and he felt "aware."

"Well, I got absolutely zip," I repeated.

"Don't worry about it," Connie said, "It's OK. It will work out."

At that moment, the sun burst from the horizon, and filled the room with a warm glow. Doug and Connie were supposed to go to work, but Connie was dead tired from the experience. She decided to stay and get some rest and settled into the mattress on the floor.

My eyelids were heavy and my eyes burned from the lack of sleep. I slid into bed, and like Connie, quickly fell asleep. Doug went off to work and returned a couple of hours later.

After a short nap, we rousted ourselves from slumber and headed out to breakfast. Once again, we spoke of the previous night's channeling, recalling each sequence of events. Connie made the comment that her face didn't feel quite right – her cheekbones felt out of place – and she tried to massage them into their regular position between sips of coffee.

My mind was still buzzing with excitement as we picked up the dorm room. I was sad to say goodbye after breakfast. As we parted, we promised to keep in touch.

I'm not sure how I managed to drive after all that had happened. The excitement of the conference, the soul reading by Leo Sprinkle, the intense "initiation" experience at the ranch, and finally Connie's channeling gave me plenty to think about during the long drive from Laramie, Wyoming to the Colorado Springs airport. I was filled with bliss on the flight back home to Phoenix, and the time passed quickly.

The experience had changed me. I had become something new and different and alien.

My life had taken a new turn.

Chapter 5

Life With Hynek, the Debunk Monk

When I returned to work after the conference, Hynek pulled me aside. I was in trouble – Jerome Clark told on me. I made the statement in front of a large group of pro-UFO researchers that the government knows about the worldwide UFO sightings and alien abductions. In addition, the government military complex has a partnership of sorts with aliens in exchange for technology.

Even though I enjoyed the standing ovation at the conference, I felt small under Hynek's glare.

"You have no evidence. Never repeat that," he told me.

I thought to myself, "The truth shall set you free."

Although we were fond of each other, we didn't always agree. Around the ICUFOR office, it was generally known that our government was working with aliens, hand-in-hand on many projects. The public, who have been told for almost 70 years that UFOs do not exist, needs to be told the truth. "The Powers That Be" have been working overtime to make sure that the public is not told the truth regarding extraterrestrials. But disclosure is inevitable: according to a recent poll, over 50% of the population believes that UFOs and extraterrestrial intelligent beings are real, and 8% of the population has actually seen a UFO.

As a result of a meeting between aliens and President Eisenhower, the public has been traded. For the use and study of our physical bodies (to advance the alien's new hybrid race), American military and scientists received advanced technical equipment. The government also felt they were no match for the vast galactic fleets that surround our planet. Even though the ICUFOR staff believed this "common knowledge," I never heard this from Hynek's lips.

The question we often debated at ICUFOR was how soon before full disclosure?

Hynek's remarks implied that he knew quite a lot about this topic, but unfortunately, the conversation appeared to stop dead at that point. I would egg him on and ask numerous questions. He'd answer with a snort, a smile, and look at me with a twinkle in his eye. Dr. J. Allen Hynek did not openly disclose what he had discovered about UFOs, nor did he spread disinformation.

I'd often ask if he had had his own ET experiences, but I never got an answer. He'd dismiss the question or change the subject. He never talked about it until later – and then only the one time.

"Ann Eller. J. Allen Hynek, Tina Choate, Brian Myers and attorney signing ICUFOR document"

Between the usual office chores of organizing, filing, receiving telephone calls, many people came to visit Dr. Hynek. Among them were Jacques Vallee and Willy Smith, both very close friends and colleagues.

Jacques Vallee is the perfect French gentleman. Tall, lean, handsome... I liked him a lot. We had spoken on the phone several times before meeting in person.

Vallee and Hynek respected each other, academically as well as in research, which made for the best of friends. I always had the feeling that Jacques felt he had to shelter or protect Dr. Hynek for some reason. I chalked it up to the harsh criticisms Hynek endured at the time the Blue Book project ended, and when Hynek switched camps from debunker to open-minded astronomer. Vallee may have had something to do with Hynek's change of heart.

Jacques Vallee was Dr. Hynek's protégé. They met in 1962 when Vallee attended Northwestern University. As a grad student, Vallee worked with Dr. Hynek on UFO case studies for the Air Force. Dr. Hynek was careful to not antagonize the Air Force, but Vallee often complained to Hynek about the way the Air Force handled the UFO files, and encouraged Allen to do the same.

On one of his visits, Vallee told me that he had been very upset with Dr. Hynek (Allen). In an incident in 1966, Hynek was quoted as declaring a remarkable UFO sighting in Dexter, Michigan as "Swamp Gas," which caused Vallee dismay.

"Why didn't you call me?" Vallee asked Hynek. "We could have discussed the situation and come up with a better explanation."

On March 20, 1966, Sheriff's deputies received calls from residents reporting brilliant lights in a nearby marsh. As the officers approached the light, they witnessed a football-shaped object pulsating with colored lights. It hovered for a short time over the marshland, then winked out. The following night, nearly 100 witnesses reported seeing a similar looking object in Hillsdale, 45 miles from Dexter. Hillsdale witnesses say an oval-shaped UFO hovered, zigzagged, accelerated and made ninety-degree turns for four hours before winking out over the nearby marshland.

Witnesses to this sighting included Sheriff's deputies (a group that is trained to observe and report), a Civil Defense director, a college dean and a large group of college students. These people were not run-of-the-mill UFO kooks.

Dr. Hynek was sent to investigate the incident by Project Blue Book. In a follow-up interview, Hynek said it was "general bedlam" when he arrived in Dexter. He was in the Sheriff's office in the small Michigan town while reporters waited outside, and was conflicted about what to say. He received a telephone call from Washington DC. After he hung up, Hynek called a news conference to say that some of the reports from witnesses suggest that they may have seen swamp gas, but that not all reports fit that category. He felt the case required further investigation, but it was difficult to conduct his investigations with the UFO frenzy going on around him.

The media picked up and ran with "swamp gas" in their headlines. To the government, Hynek's news conference statement sounded like "case closed." After all, the Air Force's top consultant had investigated and provided a plausible conclusion.

The people of Dexter and Hillsdale, Michigan were incensed. They pressured their representatives in Congress to stop America from thinking of them as nothing more than "the swamp gas state." It was Representative Gerald Ford, the future "appointed" president who wrote a letter to the Armed Services Committee Chairman, L. Mendel Rivers, demanding a better explanation and requested that a committee investigation of the UFO phenomena be formed.

A hearing by the Rivers committee in April, 1966 followed. And while hundreds of credible UFO witnesses could have been called to testify, the committee restricted the testimony to only Air Force representatives.

Hynek had never claimed to have seen a UFO and, when asked, said so in front of the committee. The good Doctor had his marching orders from the military. But he also took the opportunity to express his true feelings about UFOs.

He felt, as a scientist, that the phenomenon deserved careful study and that a panel (not responsible to the military) be formed of interested physical and social scientists. He had hoped that research and education would end public hysteria and the "giggle factor."

Had Dr. Hynek's recommendations been carried out, things might have turned out much better than they did. Hynek once told me that they didn't want to hear what he had to say. There remains an atmosphere in Washington and with the Air Force that UFO sightings could not and would not be corroborated.

They did not want the public to know that there was something in our skies that we couldn't control. After all, how would it look if we had to admit we had no defense against such an invasion? These craft came and went as they pleased any time of day or night. Our military jets could not out-run or over-take the UFOs. When our fastest jets came anywhere near them, they would simply disappear. To avoid mass panic, they reasoned, everything had to be kept in the utmost of secrecy.

Dr. Hynek thought that UFO research should be taken away from the Air Force and given to the universities. In response to this idea, the Congressional committee went to The University of Colorado to seek out a man they were certain would be very hard-nosed about it -- physicist Dr. Edward Condon. That was how the Condon Committee, and the famous "Condon Report" which followed, all started.

Condon had worked on top secret projects for the military before taking on the subject of UFOs, including the development of the atomic bomb and radar. Condon didn't believe in UFOs; he often said there was nothing to them. Condon wanted the military to "stop wasting taxpayer money and get out of the business of UFO research."

With this, UFO investigation just about came to a standstill. They were under instruction from the Pentagon, following the Robertson Panel of 1953, that the whole subject had to be debunked, period, no question about it. The prevailing attitude was completely negative toward the alien question.

When it was later released, The Condon Report stated that the UFOs were thoroughly investigated by scientists, and the subject was dead. The Air Force used its conclusions to officially close Project Blue Book.

(Hynek would chuckle that the aliens didn't bother to read the Condon Report, or we wouldn't have had so many UFO sightings since Project Blue Book ended in 1969.)

The famous "swamp gas" case finally pushed Hynek over the edge. From that point on, he began to look at reports from a different angle. He began to admit that some of them could be UFOs, and went on to continue his quest for really good scientific dialogue on the subject.

Dr. Hynek and Jacques flew to Paris late in the summer of 1985 for a UFO summit. Countries represented were from Russia, Japan, France, and the US. I had made the arrangements and they checked in a few times from Paris. Jacques was nervous about Allen. Always the ladies' man, Dr. Hynek had a few drinks and took one of the female attendees from Russia out to dinner. Jacques was afraid Hynek would talk, telling me, "She might be a spy!"

Dr. Willy Smith, an Astrophysicist from Melbourne, Florida, came to visit Allen to discuss their new database of high-quality UFO cases. I respected their privacy and would busy myself in another area either outside, in the kitchen, or the office when they were talking nearby. I could catch snippets of the conversation.

Hynek was astounded that the military could keep UFOs secret. Even with multiple witnesses, calls to sheriffs and police officers go unanswered, the FAA ignores the menacing objects over the rooftops, the military stands down while we could be invaded, and scientists are derelict in curiosity needed to find an answer to this mystery.

Smith would nod to Hynek and add his own remarks. They wondered where the media was when there were multiple reliable witnesses of the highest caliber. They considered the media's "utter indifference to UFO sightings quite pathetic." It seemed to them that everyone had a great desire to do nothing. If there were sightings, the Air Force would call all the UFOs "airplanes in formation," or a "weather eddy." Smith felt that people should all know the truth about UFOs. Hynek agreed.

Willy Smith and Dr. Hynek looked a lot alike, and they thought alike too. I dubbed them the Cosmic Twins.

My duties at ICUFOR included answering the sightings hotline phone and answering witnesses' letters. I spoke with and wrote to people who called in to report sightings or abduction experience.

The government gave little thought about the people who reported seeing UFOs or experiencing alien abductions. Marriages were broken and lives were ruined. Some people were committed to psychiatric wards and psychiatrist couches for "seeing things that weren't there." But every report had to be ridiculed and dismissed. Even though Hynek had strong opinions that the cases be further studied, he had to tow the Air Force line in order to collect his paycheck.

I had always felt Hynek had played an integral part in the government's UFO cover-up and the debunking of honest and credible witnesses. He had been the mouthpiece for the Air Force, telling people they didn't see what they saw. Allen was trying to rectify this past disbelief by creating CUFOS and ICUFOR. He hired me to do the job of making witnesses feel as though their experience had validity, and show them that we were interested and concerned.

The calls ranged from high strangeness to bizarre. One woman had little green men sitting in the tree outside her window, following a report from weeks earlier of watching a saucer hovering above her land.

Another contactee, who was in northern Arizona, thought there might be a portal to another dimension on his property and reported seeing Bigfoot and a variety of ETs.

A man from California called and claimed he could bring in the ships so Hynek could see them. Allen went out with the man one night, but no ships appeared.

I alerted Allen to all of these accounts, but did not receive much of a response. He would give me an absent-minded "hmmm," as he went back to his computer. At the time he was working in tandem with Dr. Willy Smith on a project, as well as, writing "Night Siege" with Phil Imbrogno. After making note of the sighting, these would be placed in the file for future review or passed on to a UFO researcher.

One of the long-time UFO researchers that Dr. Hynek would contact was Richard Sigismond, a psychologist and social scientist from Colorado. He also had an interest in geology and minerals and had a silver mine. Richard reported having alien experiences himself while prospecting. He would drop by to visit Allen on occasion.

The telephone lines were, of course, tapped. We didn't know who was listening in, but we had our ideas. Many times there would be a buzzing noise on the line, or the connection would break and the line would go dead in the middle of a conversation. It happened too frequently for it to be coincidence. I also began to suffer from migraine headaches that plagued me for the next ten years.

One day while I was tidying up the office, I noticed an envelope sticking out of a book. It had not been opened. The postmark was old; it was from the early 1950's. The weathered envelope was addressed to Dr. J. Allen Hynek.

"Typical," I thought to myself. Dr. Hynek was the epitome of the absent-minded professor. It would not be surprising to learn that he stuck this letter away and then forgot all about it. The return address was Ohio State University, Department of Astronomy.

I recalled how my own letter that I had sent to Dr. Hynek fell behind his desk. He hadn't seen it until nine months later.

As his secretary, I felt it was part of my job to open it.

To my astonishment, the letter stated that the sender was sending classified information to Hynek. It read:

"Intelligent signals have been received via radio telescope from the vicinity of Venus."

Adrenalin started pumping through my body -- for here was proof of intelligent life somewhere in the vicinity of Venus. This discovery was made thirty years prior in the early 1950's, and the astronomer had documented the event. In case, at such a time somebody else discovered these transmissions and did declare life on Venus, this guy had seen the transmissions first. He had sent the letter documenting this fact to Dr. Hynek to safeguard his discovery.

There had been no intention to open the letter. Dr. Hynek knew what it was at the time the letter was delivered. I didn't know what to do – so I admitted to Allen that I had opened it and apologized.

He simply took the letter and put it away. We never spoke of it again, but I felt it was a lesson for me not to pry.

On another occasion, I came upon Hynek's secret log. It was like a ledger titled "Daily Log," and was written in code. The code reminded me of the Morse code with a lot of dashes and dots. But there were also odd markings and symbols throughout the pages.

I knew Hynek classified Close Encounters into five categories:

NL: Nocturnal Lights

Nighttime lights, usually very bright, varying colors but most reports are of a yellowish orange color. The lights do not follow a path ascribable to a balloon, aircraft, satellite or a natural object. Lights seem to violate natural physical laws. About 80% of UFO sights involve nocturnal lights.

DD: Daylight Discs

These are silver, white, or metal oval objects with no point of light. They are often seen moving extremely slow or hovering. At the end of the sighting, they disappear quickly without sound. About 15% of sightings are of daylight discs.

RV: Radar-Visual UFO Reports

Objects move at a high rate of speed, but do not resemble a known weather pattern, and are observed by a radar operator. Abrupt 90-degree turns, reversals, and a formation of lights are common RV occurrences. Almost all of these cases happen at night.

CE1: Close Encounters of the First Kind

Sightings that happen close enough for witnesses to see several details. Most are brilliantly lit craft, oval or saucer shaped, lacking conventional wings, capped with a dome. These UFOs can accelerate to very high speeds, take off vertically, and silently hover.

CE2: Close Encounters of the Second Kind

Much like a CE1 experience, except the craft leaves landing traces or injuries to the witnesses.

CE3: Close Encounters of the Third Kind (Entity reports)

Having an encounter with an entity in addition to CE1 experience.

CE4: Close Encounters of the Fourth Kind (Abductions)

Witnesses report that they have been abducted for the purpose of medical examinations, and/or education. Abductees may or may not see the ship, and are often taken from cars, bedrooms, or rural areas.

Hynek used a single digit representing the kind of incident: 1 – simple sighting, 2 – physical effects, 3 – report of life form or entity, 4 – transformation of reality (abduction). Other categories were "MA" for maneuvers and "FB" for flyby. "AN" was used for other anomalies (such as unusual lights).

The log I discovered on the bookshelf was carefully marked, but not in this manner. I asked myself, "Why would Dr. Hynek be keeping a log everyday that was written in code?"

There were no words written, just dates and this code. At the time, I thought he might be working as a double agent. (We, who are in the UFO community, are incurably suspicious.)

Considering the life on Venus letter incident, I never mentioned it to him. I returned the log book to the shelf and never asked about it. I never got an answer to my question.

One of the things we at ICUFOR sponsored was a UFO Conference at the Scottsdale Civic Center. We had John McCall's Space Art exhibit, the Crystal Skulls, and the abductee Travis Walton. Dr. Hynek was a featured speaker and gave a lecture to a crowd of nearly 300 people. (I remember my girlfriend saying she was disappointed in Hynek's talk because she thought he skirted the UFO topic and never committed to any conclusions.)

Travis Walton's abduction experience is the subject of the 1993 movie, "Fire in the Sky." He was a quiet, shy, young man and had brought along his wife and baby. He spoke and answered questions about his experience of being picked up in the northern Arizona forest and returned 5 days later. His friends were concerned for his safety and swore that he was taken by an unknown aircraft. The local lawman suspected a murder cover-up and the men with Travis were nearly arrested until they passed lie detector tests.

When Travis mysteriously returned, he was obviously quite shaken up. The experience onboard the ship was frightening to him. He was subjected to physical examinations and felt as if he were being held as a prisoner. The event was still raw and fresh in his mind, and still difficult for him to talk about it.

Most people did not know that Dr. Hynek was deeply interested in metaphysical subjects. He was also a closet Rosicrucian, a member of a secret order founded in 17th Century Europe and loosely tied in with the Freemasons. In his living room hung a large oil portrait of himself wearing a ring with a large cross on his left hand. It is the same cross that is associated with the Knights of Malta. It is also the same cross I saw as a vision in the sky.

The Maltese cross is a sign of the "Christian Warrior." It was a symbol used by a group of Monks who decided to dedicate their lives to service at a hospice in the Holy Lands. But like the swastika, if traced back far enough, it seems to be extraterrestrial in origin. Swastikas and this cross reportedly have been seen on ET craft. Perhaps it is the new age symbol for "Cosmic Warrior."

In the time I spent with Dr. Hynek, I found him to be a very quiet, gentle, and extremely private man. He was reserved, never speaking much. He'd listen intently and dispensed limited feedback. He simply did not divulge what he knew. He was a master at talking in circles, generalities, and hypotheticals. When I asked him questions about UFOs and aliens, most of the time he left me up in the air. He had a good sense of subtle humor.

The ICUFOR office was a real "rag-tag" outfit. Brian Myers, Tina Choate and I had our own extraterrestrial experiences and found this topic of utmost interest. We believed that we were there to meet and greet all visitors – including those from outer space!

Tina was a pretty girl with long curly blonde hair, slender build, and a bright smile. She had a pet bird that use to roam the condo and attack my ankles under the desk. That bird and I had some karma! Tina was always suggesting ways that Brian could do things better and encouraged him to do her bidding. He was a nice guy, good looking, and worried after Tina. They were a striking couple with a lot of energy focused on Hynek and the whole UFO scene. They had many friends who would pay their bills and furnish them with whatever they needed. In return, Brian and Tina would introduce their star-struck friends to Dr. Hynek and let them hang around the office.

In those early days, Brian, Tina, Hynek, and I had many good times together. Allen's wife, Mimi, traveled a good deal visiting family, so Tina and I would cook for the four of us. We would spend evenings together just relaxing. Our days were often filled with having all kinds of people dropping in unannounced to inquire about Hynek's latest research, looking for any news.

Dr. Hynek continued to keep busy with radio, magazine, and TV interviews and enjoyed a lot of press. One of his claims to fame was his consulting with director Stephen Spielberg, and the fact that he coined the title of the movie, "Close Encounters of the Third Kind." (When Hynek gave proprietary rights to Spielberg for the use of the term, he was paid an embarrassingly low sum for doing so.)

ICUFOR did not get a lot of money. Hynek used to say that nobody would give a dime for serious UFO research. But if we were to cross the line of professional ethics and pretended we had the answer and told people UFOlogy was the cure to all their spiritual anxieties, we could raise a million dollars almost immediately.

Hynek received financial support from his interviews, books, articles, and lecture fees. Geoffrey, a well-to-do British gentleman from Las Vegas, was instrumental in persuading Hynek to move to Arizona. Geoffrey made Allen an offer he could not refuse. Mimi once told me that she and Allen never thought it would be possible to retire to such a lovely home in Scottsdale, Arizona.

I threw a party for Allen's 75th birthday at my condo. I gave him the book, *The Path of the Masters*, by Julian Johnson. It was a book that was helpful to me when I needed spiritual guidance. He read the book with a highlighter in hand, and wrote comments in the margins. After he passed away, Mimi returned the book to me. Allen and I had many discussions about spirituality, karma, reincarnation, transmigration, God, and related topics.

"J. Allen Hynek at his 75ᵗʰ birthday party"

However disorganized we were at ICUFOR, we made up for it in enthusiasm under the guidance of Dr. Hynek.

Not long after I began working at ICUFOR, Allen was diagnosed with prostate cancer. Everyone was devastated, but we encouraged him to have aggressive treatment, and to stay positive. He traveled to Barnes in St Louis for an evaluation by a specialist and received a new type of treatment. Eventually the cancer metastasized to the brain and he went to San Francisco to see specialists there.

As Allen became weaker and less focused on the research, the office slowly came to a standstill.

Over the latter months I began to lose trust of the other two in the office. It became clear to me that their welfare was far more important to them than Allen's. When I confided my feelings to Hynek, he said, "Oh, well. Maybe we just have karma together." I learned much later that Hynek cut all ties with Brian and Tina before he died.

Funds at ICUFOR grew short and the promised infusion of money never materialized. Dr. Hynek, who was battling this grave illness, did little UFO research. With no further funds coming in, I returned to my job as a nurse at the hospital in October. I left with a heavy heart. Allen and I had a close friendship.

I was staying at my daughter's home in California that spring, awaiting the birth of my first grandchild when Allen passed away. Mimi called me with the sad news, but it was a relief to know he wasn't suffering any longer.

Allen was born in 1910, during the passing of Haley's Comet. Like Mark Twain, Dr. Hynek knew when the comet came back around 76 years later, he would go out with it. This is exactly what transpired. Dr. Joseph Allen Hynek passed away on April 27th, 1986, in the year of the comet.

I was always teasing (and sometimes begging) Allen to tell me about his own paranormal experiences. He would just grin and brush off the subject. On the last visit I had with him before he died, he looked at me very intently and said, "I want you to know that I have had my own UFO experiences!" It was his parting gift to me.

Recently, I consulted with a well-known psychic medium, Marisa Ryan, to contact Dr. Hynek on the other side of the veil.

His first message to me was "be careful." He thanked me for everything I did, saying we were like "two peas in a pod." By helping him with the office correspondence and telephones, I took a big load off his shoulders.

Of course, I already knew this. Hynek and I were fond of each other and I believed we had made a connection beyond the grave.

Marisa conveyed a message that I should try to get copies of documentation left behind from a younger male, perhaps Hynek's son.

He reminded me that we had had many hours together talking about my alien experiences -- many of which I have included in my book.

He relayed through Marisa that his suspicions have all been corroborated by the Aliens he speaks to now.

He made reference to a landing in Alaska currently and said there would be activity around the Cathedral in Sedona.

He gave some personal messages to a couple of people in the UFO field. He said there are several interviews of him that haven't been published and these will reveal new information.

I asked Allen if he "walked both sides of the street," if he had been a double agent (meaning both for the government and for the common man) as I had suspected. He confessed through the medium that indeed he had, corroborating my suspicions.

He had never left his position with the government and the military – that side of him went underground with Project Blue Book.

He is well and enjoying the freedom on the other side but does wish he was still with us for there was more he wanted to expose. He said he would be a louder voice.

There was more to the connection but the rest will remain untold.

I have learned so much by working with Dr. Hynek at ICUFOR. What information I take away indicates that where we have grown technologically, we have not grown spiritually. Earth is considered a dangerous planet and jeopardizes others in our galaxy. I learned that there is a conspiracy to keep the public "under control," and we are kept from advancing spiritually and economically by "The Powers That Be." Religion is regularly used to control the masses. History is not accurate; the true history of ET contact is yet to be written.

For decades, alien Beings have been working with our subconscious minds, and they are about to welcome us into a true Brotherhood as equals in the Galaxy.

The alien presence is here for our benefit and no one should be afraid of them. Fear is the weapon the ruling force uses to keep the hoi-polloi in line.

It is time for a great awakening. Humans are in the process of transforming spiritually, moving up the ladder to new dimensions. We are headed for much excitement as this great event unfolds.

I know that I've a lot of help all around me to see that I am successfully on "my path." Thus begins a new chapter in my spiritual life.

Chapter 6

On the Road of Spirituality

Working with Dr. Hynek provided a more intimate insight into all that related to spirituality and UFOs. Within the next decade, we will be working closely with Extraterrestrials who have come to help us. Each person alive today, whether they know it or not, are in the process of deciding their spiritual fate. We are waking up from a long spiritual sleep.

I have always been interested in angels, gods, churches, cathedrals, synagogues, convents, ascended masters, ethereal Beings, and heaven. I love books and movies about these subjects, knowing the stories actually held a key to higher consciousness.

When I first began on the road of spirituality, I tried my hand at automatic writing. I would sit with a pad and pencil and wait for something or someone to move my hand. I would anticipate receiving profound truths and guidance. What I received was "Come up, come up."

Those were the only two words I wrote. I knew what the message meant; we are all going to "come up." We are all at the launch pad for a trip to a higher level of consciousness.

I have always enjoyed the pomp and circumstance of religion. I liked the ritual, the mysteries, the sacraments, the statues, the candles, the vestments. I was attracted to "tradition." Little did I know that one day I would be taking "lifelong vows" before a Saint, a Param Sant Sat Guru.

After nearly four years of intense UFO/Alien dreams, strange things began to happen. In my day-dreams, I would often see a dark man in a turban. I would be plagued by other dreams that may have been memories of previous lives and common themes of "devotion."

I once had a dream where I was on my knees scrubbing a cobblestone floor. I was a novice to the convent I was cleaning. My stockings had a hole in them and I was thankful that I had socks and shoes. Water splashed across my soiled feet. I wore the vestments of a novice because I had not yet pledged my vows to be a nun. Jesus was my savior... I awoke with a start. I could still feel the rough stones on my knees, a sign of devotion.

On New Year's Day 1982, I was lounging by the apartment complex pool. My neighbor, who happened to be a psychologist, pulled up a chaise lounge and we began to talk about meditation.

"I'm hearing other-worldly music in my right ear when I meditate," I told her, "and sometimes I hear it as I drift off to sleep."

She told me about her Guru in India, and asked if I would be interested in reading about him. "Yes," I told her. She brought me two books that same afternoon.

The first book I opened showed a photograph of the living Saint. I was stunned when I looked into his eyes. Here was the man that came to me both in my dreams and in meditation! Every word in the book resonated with me. Bells went off inside of me. I couldn't put the books down.

I recalled an earlier promise I had made to myself: "If there is a being like Jesus alive today, I'm going to find him!" There he was – looking back at me from a glossy color photo, The Master, Maharaj Charan Singh Ji.

When I found the Sant Mat Path and the Master, I became much more aware of myself. I knew that I needed to be the best person I could possibly imagine, as pure and innocent as a child before God. I had some cleaning up to do and the Master would help. He is a living saint of the highest order.

I read both books voraciously. I found my spiritual questions were being answered in a sensible, straight-forward manner. By the time I had completed the books, I decided to write to the Master and ask for Initiation.

The Master Maharaj Charan Singh Ji answered my letter personally. "It is good you want to be initiated in Sant Mat (Path of the Saints)" it read. He also cautioned me that I must fulfill two pre-conditions:

1) That my faith be based upon intellectual conviction resulting from deep and careful study of the Sant Mat books, and

2) Have the willingness and ability to accept Sant Mat regimen on food, drinks, and sex life. This ability is judged from a six-month trial period to experience this path and way of life before vows are spoken.

The Master gave me instructions to contact his nearby representative to receive Initiation. I wrote back and asked to be permitted to receive Initiation from him personally in India.

He answered, "You are as much the charge of the Master when initiated in your own country as you are the charge when initiated in India. Please have no misgivings."

I promised to make a sincere effort to live my life in accordance to the vows:

1) Vegetarian Diet: The eating of meat creates heavy karma and the point is to lighten the load, not add to it. No meat or meat byproducts. No eggs, as the "potential life" tissue lowers the natural vibrations of man when consumed.

2) Lead a good, clean moral life: No sex outside of marriage, however, the Guru encourages all to have a healthy, happy marriage. Treat others with respect. Follow the golden rule, "Do unto others as you would want them to do unto you." Be fair in all of your dealings and earn an honest living.

3) No alcohol or mind-altering drugs: Under the influence one does things which result in heavy karmic debt. Intellect, judgment, and discrimination are destroyed.

4) Meditate for 2 ½ hours every day: Give 1/10th of your time to God in meditation. The Master says, "It is meditation alone that unites us with the Guru and with God, and takes us to the highest realm of ultimate reality. Meditation should be our main concern, and this should never be sacrificed to anything of this life."

I followed the vows and found the representative in my part of the country. After the six-month trial, I applied for Initiation and filled out all the forms. I anxiously awaited an answer from the Master.

In a short time, I received a telephone call from the Master's representative informing me that the Initiation would soon take place.

The goal is to do what is required in this life so that we will not have to be born again into this lower realm. The Master promises to see us all the way home within four lifetimes at the most.

One of the mysteries of this divine path is that the Master and the Disciple must both be in a physical body for the Initiation to take place. It is a touch of the soul of the Master to the soul of the disciple.

The disciple is fine-tuned to be able to hear the "inner sound current," which is known by many names: the Holy Ghost, the Shabd, the divine melody, and the music of the spheres. By listening to this sound, the soul is purified, lifted up and pulled like a magnet into the higher regions of consciousness. It is a spiritual journey back to "the source."

My Initiation and entrance onto the Path of the Saints was given on May 1, 1982. It was a dreary evening full of dark grey clouds full of rain, but my heart was singing. I felt this was the most significant moment of my life. But there was a greater moment to come.

I haven't been 100% perfect with these vows, but I always feel love and forgiveness. The Master frequently reminds us that we are all struggling souls. We have the ideal in front of us and even if we fall, we fall with our face toward God.

Early in my practice of daily meditation and long before my Initiation with the Master, I began to have unusual experiences and visions. One time, my head spontaneously tipped backward and the word, "Yahweh," erupted from my throat.

I have a vivid memory of sitting inside my head meditating on a candle flame with another person doing the same directly across from me.

Another time, an Indian man with a turban, like my dream, walked up to me. I later discovered that this man was my Guru.

Abraham Lincoln appeared to me and pointed his finger directly at me. It reminded me of the pointing finger in the "Uncle Sam Wants You" recruitment poster. I so hoped that I hadn't been the one who assassinated him.

My third eye opened to see a dark haired man in a white robe. He was kneeling before an altar, illuminated by a single beam of light. I knew intuitively that I was watching an Initiation ceremony.

When my third eye opened during meditation on another occasion, I saw a beautiful bronze man from Atlantis.

The spring following my Initiation, I was permitted to visit the Dera community in Beas, Northern India, home of the Master.

When I arrived, the rooms were filled with disciples from all over the world. It was wonderful to attend Darshan with the Master. Love emanated from him like an aura of peaceful energy. He was different from anyone I have ever met.

He smiled and looked directly into my eyes. "Sister, do you have anything you want to tell me?"

(I had played this moment over and over in my mind. I always had dissolved into a puddle of tears.)

There was so much I wanted to say, but the only thing that escaped from my lips was, "Please forgive me."

"Is there anything in particular you have in mind?" he asked me.

I replied, "No, just everything." A single tear slid down my cheek.

I sat so close to him that I could see the roll of his tongue as he spoke. "You may ask me any questions you'd like at the evening meetings."

The next meeting I asked, "Master, aren't there Beings on other planets that have the same opportunity for spiritual advancement as we have here on Earth?"

"Yes," came his simple reply.

As my travels in India came to a close, I sat at my Master's feet. I recall how he seemed to have a golden glow and I asked him if it were possible for a disciple to see the radiant form of the Master without going inside to the inner regions.

He said, "It is so."

"Master," I intoned, "it is very difficult for me to leave you. Is there something you can say to me that will make the parting easier? Some words of encouragement?" I choked on my tears as the words poured forth. Deep down I was hoping he would tell me that I could stay with him forever.

"This place, Dera, is just bricks and mortar. It is the love here that you feel. Take this love with you and live in it. The Master is always with you."

Later, I was alone on the roof of the Western Guest House staring up at the inky sky sparkling with millions of diamond-studded stars. I remember thinking how beautiful the Indian sky looked at night.

All at once, a black mass, barely visible, moved over Dera and blocked out the stars. As it silently slid past overhead, I could not believe that I was being gifted with a sighting here halfway around the world. It wasn't easy to make out a definite shape, only a moving, silent mass of black.

I got the message from my Master that not only did aliens exist, he was showing me that they even fly over his home.

I sent him my gratitude for this experience.

I was practicing the Sant Mat spiritual lifestyle during the time I worked with Dr. Hynek. I was in this heightened sense of consciousness at the time I went to the conference in Wyoming. I was living in grace, mindful of my spiritual lifestyle when I had that profound experience with the Sisters of Light.

As Connie morphed into each Being, I could feel their love so strongly that it brought tears to my eyes. They were very powerful Beings of Light from a higher dimension. The feeling stirred my heart and soul and was simply overwhelming. It helped me to develop a universal love; I now recognize the divinity in each and every conscious being. I see the connection we all have with one another.

Since that first encounter with my Sisterhood of Light, there have been many subtle changes in me. They have not communicated to me as you and I are accustomed to. There has been little telepathic conversation. Since that first time, I have only seen one of them one time.

On the morning of my birthday, about three weeks after returning to Phoenix from Wyoming, I was sitting in meditation when all of a sudden, and as clear as a bell, they said, "Happy Birthday, Ann." It was a true telepathic experience. The words were crystal clear and I heard them inside my head. There was no way that kind of communication could be mistaken or garbled. There was no need for any translation. It was a precise and clear, "Happy Birthday, Ann." I was thrilled and patiently waited for more. None came.

Many years later, I was waking up from an afternoon nap on the couch in the living room and in my half-altered state of consciousness and with eyes wide open, I saw one of the Sisters standing by the fireplace. She was wearing a long gown and had long brunette hair with flowers or ribbons in it. When she saw that I was awake, she said, "Hi Ann." That was all and then she was gone.

Then recently in Sedona, where I currently reside, three of the Sisters came in as I was having a psychic reading. The room became electrified with their energy and both the psychic and I stopped talking. We both felt the blissful energy of love and peaceful vibrations that they were emanating.

They spoke briefly through the psychic. When we tried to get a name of where they were from, the psychic was spirited away past many planets and through other galaxies. They impressed upon her that they were from many places and dimensions. Then they gave me a personal message about the work I had accomplished.

What has happened to me over these years since the Wyoming experience is what I call a sharpening or a honing of my discrimination. It's almost as though a filter has been placed inside of me and I can recognize the nuggets of truth. My intuitive senses have become quite sharp and I seem to "know" much more than before. I can sense the vibrations that people carry with them. I see into the spirit world.

My bedroom has become a living vortex for travelers from other dimensions. I have had four specific visitations. One night just as I was about to fall asleep, a woman walked right through the bedroom wall from the driveway. My bedroom is on the second floor. It startled me so that I sat bolt upright in bed and said, "Jesus Christ!" But by then she had vanished.

About a month later, a man walked right out of the television set as I was watching a program. Again, this took place in my bedroom. He just walked right out of the TV and vanished.

The third experience was waking from a dream in the middle of the night to find a large rabbit dressed in clothes standing by the side of my bed. At least my first impression was that of a dressed rabbit (like Harvey). But as I became more awake, I could see that it was a man dressed in a red and white striped shirt, stiff white collar and cuffs and wide suspenders.

I thought, "If you only had a straw hat you could join a Barber Shop Quartet."

I sat up and said, "Do you have something to tell me?"

He gave no reaction.

I asked him, "Is there something you want from me?"

He still did not move.

Then I asked, "Why are you here?"

Before I could finish speaking, he slowly faded away.

The fourth occurred one night as I awoke from a dream to see three people standing quite close together by the side of the bed, looking at me intently and smiling. I got the distinct feeling that they were family and very happy that I could see them. After a few seconds they vanished.

These experiences have not been frightening at all. For many years I have seen sparkles of light out of the corner of my eye. Sometimes these flashes are as strong as a photographer's flash bulb. I often see movement around me and if I concentrate, a form will begin to take shape.

I feel as though the Sisters, the Ancient Ones, impress knowledge that I need into my awareness. I am thrilled to know that they have always been with me and will stay with me.

I can read a channeled piece of work and know whether the information coming through is truth or not. I have found that the information coming through Nancy Lieder on Zetatalk.com is mostly accurate. By browsing through her archives, you can see for yourself that it is an encyclopedia full of truth. There are several articles regarding survival, safe locations, and other tips in preparation for the passing of Planet X posted on the website.

The Sisterhood of Light also use my dreams as a way to effectively communicate with me. I also keep a dream log as I continue to have UFO alien dreams, and dreams full of visions of the disasters on the horizon. I can feel the UFOs hovering above my home.

I have always felt that I've been in contact with the divine. When I was six, I was totally enamored with a portrait of Jesus. When I was about 13 years old, I saw the smiling faces of celestial Beings in the four corners of my bedroom. On that occasion, everything was in slow motion, very quiet and still. Then suddenly everything rushed past me.

I had that same vision one year later – the same feeling of slowing beyond time, the same four angels smiling at me, then it ended abruptly in a rush.

The dreams I have experienced have been illuminating. I am consistently directed to seek out information I need. This covers just about all the metaphysical subjects, including UFOs and ET visitation.

My self-taught other worldly education began in the 1960s when I began reading all the metaphysical books I could find. I started with Jeanne Dixon, and went on to Ruth Montgomery, Seth, and Edgar Cayce.

One of my dreams directed me to Stonehenge. I dreamt of a mailbox on a post out by the side of the road. On the side of the mailbox were tall capital letters spelling out STONEHENGE. The dream haunted me for days. It seemed to me that a message was there for me, but I had no clue what "Stonehenge" meant.

My curiosity found me in the library a few days later. I looked it up and read that it is a prehistoric monument focused on the sun, moon and stars. It is composed of impossibly large standing stones. It is a mystery of how it was built and its original purpose. There is a burial ground nearby that post-dates the site by thousands of years.

Reading this made me remember something from a long ago and a faraway place. I wondered out loud if I remembered a previous life as a Druid? I don't know how, but I knew in my heart why this monument was placed at that spot on the lower plains of the English countryside.

I would soon visit Stonehenge where a message was indeed waiting for me. I had been there before. Long before.

One day in the late 1970's, I was in a metaphysical bookstore, browsing the shelves for an interesting book. I made three passes around the shop, and each time around I picked up the same book and read the title. *Findhorn* was printed above a photo of a luscious garden.

I thought the last thing that would interest me would be a gardening book. Each time I picked it up, I wondered why I had done so. I put it back on the shelf and looked for something more interesting. Time and again, I would be drawn back to the *Findhorn* book. I could not leave the store without purchasing that book. Spirit simply would not let it go.

I soon found myself traveling to the Findhorn Community in Scotland for the One Earth Conference. It was here I experimented with mind-expanding drugs for the purpose of "going beyond the veil" of third-dimensional life.

I kept my eyes closed through the ritualistic experience and had a vision of seeing the evolution of humanity. First I saw ape-like creatures that slowly morphed into men. Then I saw man devolve into a cave-dwelling creature.

As a result of the many spiritual teachings and experiences, I've come to the conclusion that our purpose in life is to learn "unconditional love" for all sentient Beings. There are no boundaries, no rules, no commandments, and no creeds. There is only love.

Energy is neither good nor evil. It just is. Judgment is a product of our own minds by determining what are good/bad, right/wrong, and love/hate in this play of duality. This is consciousness having an experience. It is what it feels to be alive. We forget that we participate in the life of our own making.

After Hynek passed away, I realized that I no longer liked my job at the hospital. I wanted to make a change in my life.

A friend of mine, a Peace Corps volunteer, had just returned home from Thailand. She had a good attitude about her job and her life seemed robust. Nan told me that she was heading for Washington DC to work in the medical headquarters as a screening nurse and asked me to look into it.

This is how I became a Peace Corps medevac nurse stationed in the jungles of Washington DC. It was my job to be a case manager for Peace Corps volunteers overseas seeking medical attention.

This job was full of miracles and wonderful stories. One case involved a young male volunteer in Tonga who had nearly drowned. This young man was enjoying the warm waters of the Pacific on his day off when he was pulled underwater by a strong undercurrent. He was below the surface of the water for sometime before his friends could rescue him.

They tried life saving measures on the beach, but the young man was still unconscious. One ran to get the Peace Corps doctor who managed to get the victim to the hospital by continuing life support manually by ambu bag. All of the Peace Corps volunteers were lined up in the hall taking their turn pumping the ambu bag. When one volunteer tired of squeezing the bag, another came in and took over. Oxygen tanks ran low; the young man remained unconscious.

I received a call from the Peace Corps doctor telling me the situation was less than hopeful. I immediately lined up an airevac plane from Thailand to take the victim to a hospital in Australia. Then I was able to make contact with a commercial airline out of New Zealand in the Tonga area that had extra oxygen onboard.

Next I phoned the Peace Corps doctor on Tonga. They were coming to the end of the oxygen. I silently prayed for the young man as I dialed his parents to make that dreaded phone call.

Within the hour, the New Zealand aircraft landed and tanks of oxygen were rushed to the hospital. The other Peace Corps volunteers continued to pump the ambu bag to keep the young man from dying. Eventually, the airevac plane picked up the still-unconscious patient and took him to a Critical Care Unit in Queensland, Australia.

He was admitted to the ICU. It seemed everybody was praying for him: fellow volunteers, the hospital staff, his parents, and me.

Within 24 hours, he woke up, sat up, and said, "Where am I?" He didn't remember anything. He was perfectly normal and healthy. In a few days he was permitted to return to his post in Tonga.

I spoke with him, knowing I was speaking to a miracle. "You must have a special mission in life," I told him.

While working for the Peace Corps in Washington, DC, I lived in the famous Watergate Apartments. My neighbor was the personal assistant to Senator Chris Dodd and Casper Weinberger seemed to always be in the elevator when I was. The day I moved in I met Bob Dole and he kindly welcomed me saying, "This is the best place to live in Washington".

During the Christmas holiday season, I had a VIP tour of the White House. I wasn't a VIP, but I had "connections." My friend, Ted, was a lobbyist and a retired Navy pilot. He knew his way around Washington and had many friends. Ted was my connection to a VIP tour of the White House.

As I strolled through the magnificent mansion, brightly lit with holiday decorations, I was struck with a feeling of déjà vu. I could not shake the feeling that I had been in the Red Room before, looking out the window to the South Lawn. Deep inside, I knew I had long ago looked out that very window.

As the small tour group passed the grand piano in the foyer – above which hung the portrait of JFK with his arms crossed looking pensively at the floor -- a volunteer presented holiday cards signed by the President and Mrs. Clinton to each one of us.

As the volunteer handed the card to me, I said, "You have got just about the best job in Washington!"

She smiled in agreement.

As I walked down the circular drive to the gate, I looked back at the house and said, "I've got to be involved here."

Tomorrow I would begin my quest to land a job in the White House.

"Ann Eller outside West Wing of White House"

I met Rebecca at the Peace Corps office, and she just happened to be a volunteer at the White House. She worked in the evenings in the Presidential Correspondence office. Even though the application process was closed at the time, she agreed to check with her supervisor to see if they would accept me.

She returned with an application and said I would have to have an FBI background check. I dutifully filled out and submitted all the appropriate forms. The only thing left was the background check.

I was somewhat nervous that I would not be approved due to my interest in UFOs and my association with Hynek and ICUFOR. But as fate would have it, I was issued a badge and ushered into the Executive Office Building next door to the West Wing of the White House. The Vice President, Al Gore, had an office in the building. On the main floor was a large sorting area designating President Clinton's correspondence.

Rebecca and I would go over to the White House after our day ended with the Peace Corps. We'd work until 9 pm, opening letters, reading, and sorting them according to subject. We kept our eye out for "touching" letters that the president should see. We'd set aside the letters that were thanking or praising the Clinton administration. We were also instructed to watch for threatening letters. These were handled by only one corner and carefully slipped into a plastic sleeve to be sent to the FBI. Thankfully, there were not many of these.

I applied for a position in the Visitor's Office in the East Wing. I loved working with the visitors and helping with tours through the White House. I took a leave of absence from the Peace Corps while they moved to a new office, and worked full time in the Visitors Office.

Then my third and final position was in the Social Office. Here I spent most of my time inviting dignitaries, cabinet members, congressmen and regular Americans to gala functions at the White House.

All of the White House volunteers were invited to President Clinton's birthday party on the South Lawn. We each had an opportunity to shake the President's hand and wish him well. This was on a Friday, and he was scheduled to be deposed on the matter of Miss Monica Lewinsky the following Monday. Miss Lewinsky had an intimate relationship with President Bill Clinton. In a nationally televised White House news conference, Clinton stated, "I did not have sexual relations with Monica Lewinsky."

I shook his hand and looked him right in the eye. "Good luck on Monday, Mr. President."

He gave me a cocky smirk and said, "Oh that oughta be fun."

Clearly, the message remains that we want honesty from our leaders, no matter how shocking the circumstances. As a country, we have become utterly exasperated with politician's sexual issues.

I like to believe that the whole country learned from this episode. (Besides what the meaning of "is" is.) I like to think that this fiasco forced the country to look at its leaders in all honesty. We have to ask ourselves, "When are we going to vote for those who are spiritually-oriented and morally sound?"

"Ann Eller and President Bill Clinton"

*"Ann Eller with Troy Donahue and other
White House Staff"*

I traveled to Jamaica, Honduras, Costa Rica, and Nicaragua for the Peace Corps. Once I got on a crowded elevator at the hotel in Honduras, and could see an Uzi inside the jacket of the man next to me. In these countries, shoot-outs would regularly and spontaneously erupt, so I always had to be vigilant. Seeing their world as an observer, I felt sorry for the people who felt they had to live this way.

Human life is sacred and it's extremely important to our cosmic family. We belong to the same spirit family; our spirit was born of the stars. Our souls were born of the one source of life in the universe. Our coverings may be different but we are all one family in Spirit.

The experience of living in this third dimensional reality is only part of our existence. We are really multidimensional personalities, dwelling in many dimensions, and simultaneously.

In the book *Seth Speaks*, Jane Roberts wrote, "Your concept of reality as seen through your physical senses, scientific instruments, or arrived at through deduction, bears little resemblance to the facts – the facts are difficult to explain."

"Your planetary systems exist at once, simultaneously, both in time and space. The universe that you seem to perceive, either visually or through instruments, appears to be composed of galaxies, stars, and planets, at various distances from you. Basically, however, this is an illusion. Your senses and your very existence as physical creatures program you to perceive the universe in such a way. The universe, as you know it, is your interpretation of events as they intrude upon your three-dimensional reality. The events are mental. However, this does not mean you cannot travel to other planets."

Our minds can influence matter because thought creates form. We are very powerful Beings creating our own reality.

We have lived many lives and in many places. We are all star travelers, we have all been alien. There is knowledge held within ourselves that we are not consciously aware of.

The wars and terrors of the wars are financed by our fears. We can create a glorious earthly experience or hell on Earth. While we receive many messages from celestial Beings or channeling from aliens, we must not go forth with only blind faith. The message is not about religion, but rather knowing that we need understanding of the worlds beyond the stars in order to grow spiritually. God's kingdom is far more vast than we can even imagine.

In order for spiritual growth to occur, we must be as human as possible. The Master is the Ultimate Perfect Human. This is a new age of enlightenment. To see where we are going, we must know where we are now and where we have come from. We are wired for advancement, and at the appropriate time we will be reminded of our true nature.

The human purpose is to evolve into higher consciousness, in higher dimensional planes. The basic vibrational centers of the body, the "chakras" help us to align mind, spirit and body into one "Christ Consciousness."

My philosophy is that we are here to realize our dreams and passions and in doing so, we automatically travel our destined Path back to the source of all creation.

Like the Bhavacakra, the Tibetan Wheel of Becoming, our existence is a continuous cycle of birth, life and death. We escape this wheel by enlightenment, by returning to the source with guidance from the Perfect Living Master.

Only the inner sound current, the WORD of GOD, is real and everlasting, everything else changes and dies.

Extraterrestrials regularly visit planet Earth. But it is against a universal law for them to interfere with our development. For this reason, they are most often in a higher dimension and invisible to us.

They monitor us and "drop in" occasionally before disappearing back into a different dimension.

However, at the present time we are surrounded by massive numbers of spacecraft and extraterrestrials and have many of them living with us and walking amongst us.

Our political leaders with the "secret government" are dangerously close to losing their concept of what is important in their spiritual world. They are like the familiar "Greys" who lack a human emotional body. Our leaders need love, forgiveness, and a moral compass. Currently we are entering the time of the "Harvest". We are being separated into the wheat and the chaff. Will you choose transformation to a higher spiritual level or will you choose to stay in the third dimension?

Sentient life exists both on countless physical worlds as well as other dimensions; it is necessary to help each other in order to help ourselves.

While individual belief and faith guide us spiritually, the UFO phenomenon has immense spiritual implications. The bottom line is that it's time to wake up and grow up. We must listen to our own "knowing." And we must remember to discern the truth for ourselves.

At this time, many cycles are coming to an end. It is also time for the return of the Planet called "Nibiru," commonly known as Planet X. All of this contributes to a perilous time for us, and a time when spiritual values will be tested.

Chapter 7

The Government, Planet X, and the Shift

Planet X has crossed Earth's path a multitude of times since time began. It is documented by ancient myths from all over the globe and is known by many different names. To the ancient Sumerians, it is called "Nibiru," to the Egyptians, it is called "the Destroyer," and Druid ancestors of the Celts call it "the Frightener."

Zecharia Sitchin, author of several books presenting his interpretation of many early Sumerian tablets, has studied ancient literature for more than 35 years. Following is condensed information that has been researched extensively by Sitchin over many years. According to Sitchin's works, mankind's history may have been shaped by otherworldly contact. The 12th planet, Nibiru, is on a wide parallax orbit, taking it far into space, beyond our sight. It returns into view about every 3,600+ years and, according to Sitchin, it is due to return sometime in 2060. Other sources say Planet X will return to view before 2012 and in the book *When the Sun Darkens* by Jason Breshears, Nibiru's predicted arrival is around 2040.

Ancient texts say Planet X will be seen coming from the sun and it appears as large as the moon and writhes like a dragon due to its tail of asteroids, moons, and space debris whipping in the sky. This is the vision of the dragon flipping its tail in the sky I saw in Wyoming.

Mother Shipton, (1488-1561 lived during the time of Henry VIII of England) speaks of a "fiery dragon" that will be seen by man two times (coming in to the solar system, and going back out again).

She says that this will cause two sets of natural disasters and the second will be worse than the first.

"A fiery dragon will cross the sky six times before this Earth shall die. Mankind will tremble and frightened be for the sixth heralds in this prophecy. For seven days and seven nights man will watch this awesome sight. The tides will rise beyond their ken to bite away the shores and then the mountains will begin to roar and earthquakes split the plain to shore."

She continues by indicating that once the "fiery dragon" and Earth settles down, mankind will try to return to the way things were and carry on in the usual way.

She then speaks of the second visit: "His masked smile - his false grandeur, will serve the Gods their anger stir. And they will send the dragon back to light the sky - his tail will crack upon the Earth and rend the Earth and man shall flee, King, Lord, and serf. But slowly they are routed out to seek diminishing waterspout. And men will die of thirst before the oceans rise to mount the shore. And lands will crack and rend anew you think it strange, it will come true."

Nancy Lieder, a contactee and Emissary for those from Zeta Reticuli, channels this information at the ZetaTalk.com website:

"Consider that the sequence of events we have described during the last weeks have many points where catastrophes will occur. Planet X and the Earth are also at various positions in the sky, vis-a-vis each other, during these events. The severe wobble, lean to the left, and lean away into the 3 days of darkness for the northern hemisphere will cause earthquakes and tidal waves and panic. This is the time frame Mother Shipton is referring to for the first set of catastrophes. We have stated that the Planet X complex will be visible in the sky during the last weeks, and depending upon how close the planet and the Earth are to each other, may be seen as directly blocking the Sun (as in the last week) or off to the side as a Second Sun. If the angle between Planet X and the Earth is not sufficient, Planet X is lost in the glare of the Sun, and thus may seem to disappear, temporarily. After the 3 days of darkness and 6 days of sunrise west (somewhat to the west of the North Pole), the Earth will return to its upright position but will gradually slow and stop in its rotation. The Earth, during this time, is drawn toward Planet X, many millions of miles closer, and during this time the Planet X complex will of course appear dramatically larger. The pole shift, which will then occur, is the most traumatic of all."

Several prophets have predicted a pole shift during our current era. Edgar Cayce, the sleeping prophet, said: "Where there has been a frigid or semi-tropical climate, there will be a more tropical one, and moss and fern will grow." It seems that landmasses will move thousands of miles to different climate zones. Earth will seemingly lie on its side, and natural cataclysms of biblical proportions unlike we've ever seen will strike.

When Planet X last appeared, it was the time of the Exodus when Moses led the Jews out of Egypt. The plagues during that time were part of a global catastrophe, and following the Exodus, Egypt had to fight off a massive invasion from the south. The pantheon of gods failed to save the Egyptians, and the once mighty nation fell.

The Exodus occurred because of the problems being caused by Planet X. Slave masters were devastated and distracted and did not think about their slaves. The Jews left after a long night, horrendous earthquakes, and volcanic eruptions. The government fell and guards left their posts leaving chaos in their wake. The household servants stole from their masters and crept away in the seemingly never-ending night. The rulers held their heads in worry and discussed amongst themselves how they might placate the gods. It wasn't until the Earth's rotation was re-established that order was restored.

This was also the time of the giants, the crossbred offspring of aliens and humans. In Sitchin's The Earth Chronicles series, he translates the Sumerian myths of an ancient alien race called the Annunaki who landed on Earth over 300,000 years ago.

During an alien civil war, Alalu, the ruler of Nibiru, was overthrown and fled to Earth. Here he found gold – an element Nibiru needed to stabilize its rapidly depleting atmosphere. Aliens came for the gold, but the mining of it was hard work. The aliens revolted against having to do the hard manual labor. The Annunaki leaders decided to create a slave race of Homo sapiens who were taken to the "cradle of civilization" in Mesopotamia. Here human civilization was born.

"Annunaki," or "Those who from heaven to Earth came", as the Sumerians called them, stood an average of 8 feet tall and were far heavier and were more muscular than humans. Their planet is known by many names – Nibiru, Marduk, Wormwood, the Destroyer, the Red Star, and Planet X. The Sumerians counted 12 planets as they entered our solar system, including the moon and sun as celestial bodies.

According to Nancy at ZetaTalk.com:

"There is life on the 12th Planet, the giant comet that causes the periodic pole shifts. The primary race is a humanoid race, which would be and have been considered giants by humans on Earth. There have been many excellent books written on this subject, and all hold a grain of truth.

They have a hierarchical structure. We would venture to say no true democracies as you might term them. However, there are among them intellectuals who have great compassion for their fellow creatures and fellow citizens and have great influence in their society and are revered.

The giant hominoids on the 12th Planet to this day dress in attire reminiscent of Roman soldiers. Rome in fact modeled after them, rather than these hominoids modeling after the Romans. The males find this to be comfortable attire that has a macho image. You might look to your ancient Greek and ancient Roman societies for a glimpse of their lifestyle, because these societies carried the influence of these visitors very heavily.

The giant hominoids were not grossly muscular, as mankind's over-developed muscle men are. They were and are well proportioned, with rounded muscles but without the extreme bulging that muscle men try to achieve. Nancy, who has met one, will tell you that they are extremely attractive, and proportional.

The giant hominoids had long faces, but the skulls that have been discovered and ascribed to aliens are not these giant hominoid's skulls. The Easter Island heads were designed to intimidate, as this appearance in the faces was and is indeed their facial structure.

They do not sleep, because they do not have a rising and setting sun. They have a dimmer day. The glow in their atmosphere comes from rifts within their ocean. They inhabit a brown dwarf that is in a slow smolder.

It happens also to be a water planet, so that the places where the results of the chemical reaction that produces their light come through are in the deepest rifts closest to the molten core, and scattered throughout their atmosphere. Therefore they have a continuous light, equivalent perhaps to late in your day or very early in the morning. They do have their quiet times.

Their agriculture is much less extensive than the agriculture of Earth. They tend to gather rather than grow. There are fewer of them per square mile than your rich and fertile Earth sustains.

Gold mining is occurring today on a moon of Mars, which has been approached by man's probes and subsequently shot down by these hominoids who were not about to let themselves be filmed by their former slaves. This moon, Phobos, is rich in the minerals they seek."

In Sitchin's book, *The 12ᵗʰ Planet*, the aliens realize that the return of Nibiru would cause global cataclysms and decided not to tell mankind in order to deplete their population. One of the Annunaki breaks his promise and warns Noah of the coming disaster, who builds an ark and is saved.

During the pass, Nibiru will only be 14 million miles from Earth. Nibiru is four times the diameter of Earth. Although the tail will pelt the Earth with impacts of meteors, the real threat comes from the way in which Nibiru interacts electrically and magnetically with us.

Due to the interactions between Earth and Nibiru, we'll experience super volcanic eruptions, giant 9+ earthquakes along major fault lines, and seas rising up over land for hundreds of miles. Weather patterns all over the world will become increasingly violent as summer and winter merge into a single season. Our atmosphere could become poisonous to breathe. Our power grids, transportation, communication networks could quickly become nonexistent. Lethal electrical charges could further harm life. To survive, many will take shelter in underground facilities.

NASA's Infrared Astronomical Satellite (IRAS) first sighted what many believe to be Planet X in 1983. In April 2006, a South Pole Telescope (SPT) was placed at the Amundsen-Scott South Pole Station in Antarctica to track Planet X's arrival. Thomas Van Flandern reported to the American Astronomical Society that irregularities in the orbit of Pluto indicate our solar system contained a tenth planet.

We have been tracking Planet X for twenty-seven years!
No one knows the exact timing of the Pole Shift. However, there are certain markers to watch for. These markers are clearly given on www.zetatalk.com.

When Planet X first appears it will look like a second sun by day and a fiery dragon in the night sky. The gravitational pull will cause the Earth to wobble, lean away, and cause three days of darkness for the northern hemisphere. A series of natural disasters and Earth changes including earthquakes and tidal waves will occur causing worldwide panic. After the three days of darkness, Earth will return to its upright position but will gradually slow and stop in its rotation. The pole shift will then occur with the most traumatic catastrophes imaginable.

And yet, like the topic of UFOs, our government isn't talking. The Earth changes we've experienced to date have been attributed to man-made "global warming." However, this doesn't explain why all the planets in our solar system are heating up. There are perturbations in our solar system indicating that Planet X is due to arrive at our doorstep very soon.

From ZetaTalk: "Where most discussion on the pole shift being deflected if humankind changes their ways, or some such fantasy, is based on a wish, when presented as a fact coming from government agents this is disinformation designed to get the public to ignore the Earth changes and continue to attend to their jobs and to paying their taxes. We have explained that if the Earth were peopled by souls almost exclusively in the Service-to-Other orientation, that the Earth would be moved into 4th Density and thus escape the pole shift, which is caused by a rogue planet that will remain in 3rd Density."

"We have explained that the Earth is at present only about 30% Service-to-Other and would not acquire the requisite percentage before the time of the cataclysms. However, some alien groups are so tenderhearted they cannot bear to be the bearer of bad tidings, and they have told their contactees that if mankind changed, that they could avoid the calamity. This is repeated endlessly as a fact, which it is not, as it is in fact only a partial truth."

"Since this is so prevalent on the Internet, and grasped by humankind desperate for an answer to what they perceive, accurately, as desperate times on the horizon, those wanting to keep mankind content until the last minute are talking this up as a fact of which the government is aware. It's all disinformation. All of it."

It must be strongly emphasized that, even with the best of intentions, this event will take place. If it does not happen by 2012, it could happen in 2040 or 2060. Another point to note is that not every passage of Nibiru is totally devastating. Each passage is different depending on the angles and distance between the planets and other certain conditions.

In a recent dream, I was shown the exact location of Planet X. When I awoke, I wrote it down. I went back to sleep and dreamt the very same dream again – exactly as the first time. It was like a punctuation point; it said, "Don't forget because this is important!"

In 2003, I saw Planet X for myself when it was barely visible to the naked eye. More recently in 2007, the cloud cover was just right to shield the sun's glare, and I made out a second source of light. (Planet X is also referred to as "the second sun.")

There is strain on the Earth that is gradually increasing as the interloper moves in. Electro-magnetic energy between Planet X and the Earth interact leaving destruction in its wake. The push/pull movement is felt in all the large and small tectonic plates making up the planet.

The pull of this Planet and the gravitational energy is strong enough now to pull bridges, railroads and gas lines apart. As Planet X moves closer, Earth's core heats up, heating up magma, resulting in large earthquakes along fault lines, and causing undersea volcanoes to erupt. The "ring of fire" heats up with frequent earthquakes, some registering 11 and higher. The energy moves the plates and numerous masses of land fall and are swallowed by violent seas, while other masses move upward and become new mountains and rivers. Weather is erratic causing massive crop failures. Excessive winds literally blow cities apart. Tornadoes and hurricanes increase. Fire caused by the tail of Planet X ignites homes in drought areas further depleting water sources.

In another dream vision about Planet X, I saw a giant tsunami wave quickly building in the Pacific Ocean. The ocean heaved toward the coast of California – a massive amount of water. I was driving south along the coast highway. I knew I had to get to San Diego and turn east across the desert. I was desperately trying to outrun the wave.

Then I watched from above as a huge tidal wave swept over New York City drowning everything in its wake. The waves were as high as the skyscrapers. The land was inundated far beyond the city.

Another dream, I awoke to the house being surrounded with water with no way to escape. There were small nuclear explosions going off in different cities resulting in chaos. Trauma was everywhere – I could not get away.

Last year, I heard a voice in a dream saying, "Prepare the people for nuclear war!" I have given that one a great deal of thought. How can you prepare for such a nightmare?

I think of growing up during the cold war when backyard bomb shelters were common. Today, the Zetas suggest that we dig a shallow gully open at each end, with a roof made of tin or aluminum sheeting as protection from falling fire and debris from the tail of Planet X. We are further encouraged to move to rural areas near water where we can grow our own food with a nearby water supply. Researching safe locations at Zetatalk.com, taking a survivalist-training course and a first aid class might be good ideas right now.

The most significant dream that I had in regards to this whole topic of the Earth shifting on its axis haunts me to this day. I was in a large spacecraft high above Earth. I was watching on a monitor as it spun like a big blue marble in space, when suddenly it lurched and fell over. I looked over to the astonished crowd; a whole group of survivors had been taken onboard. I was panic-stricken when I saw the oceans slosh way out into space and then wash across the planet. I couldn't believe what I had just seen. We felt sure that no one could have survived it, and the implication of this fact stunned me.

We were refugees on this alien spacecraft. We had a certain area we were permitted to be in, and other areas were off limits. Other Beings stood guard next to the entry of areas off-limits. They didn't seem menacing to me; they were simply doing their job. This was a very lucid dream.

In another dream of a large map of the United States, I learned that, like other landmasses around the globe, it is expected that the United States will change drastically during and after the shift. Gordon Michael Scallion and Ms. Toye of I AM America, each have maps of the future land changes.

These maps show where the globe is changed by the upheavals. A huge wedge of land is missing from California all the way to Nebraska. Edgar Cayce said he would reincarnate in 100 years and the coastline would be in Nebraska. Half of Florida will be under water and there will be a great waterway dividing the east from the west. The New Madrid fault line will alter the land causing the east coast to lose a lot of land. One should be at least a hundred miles inland in order to be relatively safe on any coast.

The Zetas expect that 90% of the population will perish in the coming cataclysms. You need to prepare if you wish to survive. There are safe locations and available supplies of seeds and tools to make it through. There are like-minded groups on the Internet, as well as, in your local community. Look around, talk to your friends and family, and plan ahead.

But, the most important fact to remember is, "trust yourself." Your natural intuition and spiritual guides will be giving you information and direction throughout the shift. It is your job to listen.

Hone your ability to be still and quiet within. Meditate. Ask yourself what your gut is telling you. Feel the help all around you. No one is going through this experience by himself or herself. Everyone has angels and guides who are pledged to be of assistance. It is your job to listen.

The Zetas have said the reason the Pleiadians have not talked about the coming cataclysms is because of FEAR. They say they do not want to induce Fear, but there really isn't much that can be done at this point.

Chapter 8

Prophecy From The Stars
and My Message To You

If you knew you had only a short time to live, what would you want to accomplish? How would you spend your time? Would you continue your current path, or would you change?

This Planet X prophecy of upheaval and destruction is a heads-up. We know what is coming and that we don't have much time left. However, we do have time to make amends, to tell our family how much we really love them, to ask for forgiveness and ample opportunity to right the wrongs in our lives. We have a chance to be the "loving light" that we truly are -- to rise to the occasion and help anyone in need, to be a hero, to be kind, loving and spiritual.

This is a time to open our hearts like we've never done before and stretch our spiritual "oneness" around the world. It is time to graduate to a higher level of consciousness. Wake up!

For me, going into spirit might be preferable than riding out the chaos and starting over from scratch. There will be no electricity, no computers, no iPods, no cell phones, no vehicles, no dwellings, no clean water, no pharmaceuticals and no food. The remnants of civilization will begin again at point zero, and the planet will need a period of settling down before life can flourish again.

However, our brothers and sisters from space will be nearby and will help those who survive clean up the mess and provide technology for survival. It is not their intent to rescue us, but rather to support us as we handle ourselves through this crisis.

We signed up to be here before we came into this life. Can you remember thinking, "Wow, there are going to be a lot of fireworks and I get to have a front row seat! This will be exciting!" When the veils between the worlds dropped after our birth, we forgot all about it.

You may ask, "Why aren't we hearing any of this from our leaders or our scientists? Why aren't newspapers reporting the approach of Planet X?" The government and the power elite know all about Planet X and its close passage and have kept it a secret. They have effectively threatened scientists and astronomers with their life and the lives of their loved ones just as they did with the astronauts who saw alien spacecraft. It's all part of the UFO cover-up and their refusal to disclose what they know.

"The Powers That Be" want you to go to work, pay your taxes, drink your beer, and sit in front of the television while they blindside you with "celebrity news." In the meantime, they took taxpayer money and built underground bunkers and stocked them with food and medical supplies. This is where they were planning to ride out the storm until those who were sent in to test it out died. Now they may be planning a trip to the moon instead. Too bad, you're not invited to their party. They are well armed.

We have learned that if one does well here in this third dimensional reality, and overcomes the gross temptations of greed, anger, lust, ego, and pride to help one's fellowman, there can be rapid spiritual growth. We, as spiritual Beings, have been here in a continual cycle of death and rebirth for hundreds of thousands of years.

The last time we were truly conscious was when we were hanging upside down in our mother's womb. We met with our "spiritual counselors" before we incarnated into this world in order to be placed in the life which would benefit us the most. We knew we were Beings of Light and that this realm, heavy with physical matter and dross, would weigh us down. We knew we would be made to forget who we really are, and as a result, we would make many mistakes.

There is a plan for our life, but we are made to forget it as soon as we are born. There is no end to our desires and cravings and we have to keep returning to this world in order to fulfill them. We have lived many lives and died as many times. We have had many lovers, many children, and have experienced just about everything we needed to experience. We have been there, done that – and we continue to recycle ourselves. Thus, we fall into the never-ending wheel of birth and death. The only way out is within, going in and up in consciousness.

There is no end, no finale for the soul. We were from the beginning and will be forever. There is no death. There is an end to our physical bodies, but there is no end to our life. We are energy Beings of Light and cannot be destroyed; we can only be changed.

You may already have been sensing that something important is just around the corner. The world is rapidly changing, and your own priorities have shifted. Many are feeling the urge to change physical location, jobs, or even life partners. Energy is on the move and continues to increase in speed.

Keep in mind that what is happening in the outside world is also happening within our physical, mental, emotional and etheric (energy) bodies. The only body we leave behind when we "die" is the physical body. However, all these bodies are being affected by what's happening in the outside world. We are affected by the electro-magnetic energy, which is also affecting the Earth and the cosmos.

This energy vibrates at a moderate rate of speed in this third density realm. As we move higher up in the realms, the energetic speed increases. There are many higher realms and other dimensions with more beauty and intelligence than the one in which we find ourselves.

Love is the cosmic glue that holds it all together. Usually we cannot see something or someone in a higher realm because our eyes are geared to see only in the 3rd dimension. People who are "sensitive" can often see, feel, and hear in these higher dimensions.

The whole of creation is teeming with life, with billions and billions of souls, in all different modes and in all different places. Our celestial friends in the higher realms are here en masse to give us as much help as they possibly can.

The Heavenly Spiritual Hierarchy is closer to us than ever because it has been decreed that we be lifted into the fourth and fifth dimensions. But in order for man to take this leap, we must learn to live together peacefully, recognize the divinity in others and ourselves, respect the Earth and all of its creatures, and get right with our own personal God.

My relationship with the ancient Sisters of Light, which began in Wyoming, has helped me to continue to grow spiritually. These Beings are from a higher dimension, and they had to lower their vibration and raise my consciousness in order to become visible to me. The love that poured out from them was unbelievable. It touched me so deeply in my soul that it caused the tears to flow. Even now, I can feel their love reaching out to me. It is simply overwhelming.

The same "consciousness raising vibration" holds true for extraterrestrial spacecraft. In order for us to see them, they must lower their vibratory rate. To them, lowering their vibration is like putting on a heavy diver's suit that weighs them down. For us, to be lifted in vibration and consciousness is to feel lighter, brighter, and joyful.

As we go through the process of being readied for the 4th or 5th density, the Earth is also being raised as the solar system moves up along with the galaxy into a new dimension in a new quadrant of the universe. We are currently passing through new and strange territories and are subject to the unusual energies of these places.

Many are being given a choice whether to leave the planet now, or ride it out. Each individual soul will have a choice to move forward or stay at the current 3rd dimensional reality. There is no hurry in the grand scheme of things. There is no time, so we can take as long as we like to move forward. There is no penalty or punishment if one chooses not to move forward. If one wants to experience 3rd density life over and over, it is of no consequence. Eventually all souls will go back to the one source of all creation.

Our souls descended from a very high place. God created us in order to experience all aspects of life including the good, evil, and all things in between. But we have sunk so low in the vibrational level that we have forgotten that we are God's children and the heirs to His Kingdom. It is part of the learning process to care for others and help them along the path. It is in helping that we receive our greatest aid. We are in the process of working our way back home to the highest spiritual realm; we are going back to God.

We are divine Beings, we just don't know it yet. As we raise our vibrational level, we will become more god-like until we become God in our own right. In the meantime, we have a lot of cleaning up to do to neutralize our karma. If we give out love, it returns. If we are miserable individuals, we will attract more misery and make everyone around us miserable. The karmic account of killing, raping, and pillaging must be balanced. Likewise, if we are beloved and kind and strive to help others, we will receive kindness and love in return.

God in his mercy has always sent his sons to the Earth to teach the truth to those with ears to hear. We are never without at least one Saint of the highest order. But man has molded and changed the spiritual truths to fit the likings of a few elite who would control the masses through fear. It is now time to wake up and think for ourselves. This is the time when we must own our "knowing," and not buy into the deceit and the lies of control. It is time to wake up and embrace the one true connection we all have. We must discriminate and search for the truth.

The planet is currently being cleansed, and the population will suffer. We have an opportunity to accept all the help being offered by all of the loving Beings in this sector of the galaxy. Light and energy are being beamed around the entire Earth to help wake us and reconfigure our DNA. We are being transformed into the wonderful light Beings that we really are. We are becoming "Galactic Humans."

At this time, many cycles are coming to a conclusion. Planet X's return, the economic crisis, war, and starvation, all contribute to a perilous time for the inhabitants of planet Earth. According to the Zetas (see Zetatalk.com), as Planet X comes closer to the Earth in its long elliptical orbit, the electromagnetic fields of both planets interact to cause a shift of the Earth's axis. The time quickly approaches when we will experience severe earthquakes, floods, fires, volcanic eruptions, drought, starvation, and physical death.

I feel it is in our best interest to welcome our family from the stars in this hour of need. They are not here to save all of us, but to help us during this test of our spiritual will. Many of us will cross over into spirit and begin to plan our next life's journey. Some will remain, and with the help of the visitors, begin life anew on this planet. Some will be removed and live on the spacecraft for a period of time before returning to re-settle the Earth. Our Planet, Earth, will survive and proceed into the fourth dimension. There will also be human survivors of this pole shift. If your choice is to survive then begin preparing now.

When I first tried my hand at automatic writing, I received "Come up, come up." Now, 50 years later, I realize that the message "come up" means that we are about to ascend in consciousness.

In that, I rejoice.

"In the dead of night, a Sufi began to weep.
He said, "This world is like a closed coffin, in which
We are shut and in which, through our ignorance,
We spend our lives in folly and desolation.
When Death comes to open the lid of the coffin,
Each one who has wings will fly off to Eternity,
But those without will remain locked in the coffin.
So, my friends, before the lid of this coffin is taken off,
Do all you can to become a bird of the Way to God;
Do all you can to develop your wings and your feathers."

-Attar

ABOUT THE AUTHOR

Ann Eller has had a diverse and expansive history as an elementary school teacher, ob-gyn Nurse Practitioner, gyn surgical nurse, medevac nurse for the Peace Corps, White House volunteer, worldtraveler, and secretary to the renowned astrophysicist, Dr. J. Allen Hynek.

Ann has had her own extraordinary experiences with alien visitors. In her book, *Dragon in the Sky: Prophecy From The Stars*, she tells of her astonishing experiences, her message from the stars, and her appeal to all for higher consciousness and UFO disclosure.

Her personal philosophy is that we are here to realize our passions and dreams and in so doing we are naturally following the Path back to the Source of all creation. She is the mother of two and grandmother of three and currently resides in Sedona, Arizona.

www.anneller.com

www.dragoninthesky.com

MORE TITLES FROM THE BOOK TREE 1-800-700-TREE

ORDER FROM YOUR FAVORITE BOOKSELLER OR CALL FOR OUR FREE CATALOG

Of Heaven and Earth: Essays Presented at the First Sitchin Studies Day, edited by Zecharia Sitchin. ISBN 1-885395-17-5 • 164 pages • 5 1/2 x 8 1/2 • trade paper • illustrated • $14.95

God Games: What Do You Do Forever?, by Neil Freer. ISBN 1-885395-39-6 • 312 pages • 6 x 9 • trade paper • $19.95

Space Travelers and the Genesis of the Human Form: Evidence of Intelligent Contact in the Solar System, by Joan d'Arc. ISBN 1-58509-127-8 • 208 pages • 6 x 9 • trade paper • illustrated • $18.95

Humanity's Extraterrestrial Origins: ET Influences on Humankind's Biological and Cultural Evolution, by Dr. Arthur David Horn with Lynette Mallory-Horn. ISBN 3-931652-31-9 • 373 pages • 6 x 9 • trade paper • $17.00

Past Shock: The Origin of Religion and Its Impact on the Human Soul, by Jack Barranger. ISBN 1-885395-08-6 • 126 pages • 6 x 9 • trade paper • illustrated • $12.95

Flying Serpents and Dragons: The Story of Mankind's Reptilian Past, by R.A. Boulay. ISBN 1-885395-38-8 • 276 pages • 6 x 9 • trade paper • illustrated • $19.95

Triumph of the Human Spirit: The Greatest Achievements of the Human Soul and How Its Power Can Change Your Life, by Paul Tice. ISBN 1-885395-57-4 • 295 pages • 6 x 9 • trade paper • illustrated • $19.95

Mysteries Explored: The Search for Human Origins, UFOs, and Religious Beginnings, by Jack Barranger and Paul Tice. ISBN 1-58509-101-4 • 104 pages • 6 x 9 • trade paper • $12.95

Mushrooms and Mankind: The Impact of Mushrooms on Human Consciousness and Religion, by James Arthur. ISBN 1-58509-151-0 • 103 pages • 6 x 9 • trade paper • $12.95

Vril or Vital Magnetism, with an Introduction by Paul Tice. ISBN 1-58509-030-1 • 124 pages • 5 1/2 x 8 1/2 • trade paper • $12.95

The Odic Force: Letters on Od and Magnetism, by Karl von Reichenbach. ISBN 1-58509-001-8 • 192 pages • 6 x 9 • trade paper • $15.95

The New Revelation: The Coming of a New Spiritual Paradigm, by Arthur Conan Doyle. ISBN 1-58509-220-7 • 124 pages • 6 x 9 • trade paper • $12.95

The Astral World: Its Scenes, Dwellers, and Phenomena, by Swami Panchadasi. ISBN 1-58509-071-9 • 104 pages • 6 x 9 • trade paper • $11.95

Reason and Belief: The Impact of Scientific Discovery on Religious and Spiritual Faith, by Sir Oliver Lodge. ISBN 1-58509-226-6 • 180 pages • 6 x 9 • trade paper • $17.95

William Blake: A Biography, by Basil De Selincourt. ISBN 1-58509-225-8 • 384 pages • 6 x 9 • trade paper • $28.95

The Divine Pymander: And Other Writings of Hermes Trismegistus, translated by John D. Chambers. ISBN 1-58509-046-8 • 196 pages • 6 x 9 • trade paper • $16.95

Theosophy and The Secret Doctrine, by Harriet L. Henderson. Includes *H.P. Blavatsky: An Outline of Her Life*, by Herbert Whyte. ISBN 1-58509-075-1 • 132 pages • 6 x 9 • trade paper • $13.95

The Light of Egypt, Volume One: The Science of the Soul and the Stars, by Thomas H. Burgoyne. ISBN 1-58509-051-4 • 320 pages • 6 x 9 • trade paper • illustrated • $24.95

The Light of Egypt, Volume Two: The Science of the Soul and the Stars, by Thomas H. Burgoyne. ISBN 1-58509-052-2 • 224 pages • 6 x 9 • trade paper • illustrated • $17.95

The Jumping Frog and 18 Other Stories: 19 Unforgettable Mark Twain Stories, by Mark Twain. ISBN 1-58509-200-2 • 128 pages • 6 x 9 • trade paper • $12.95

The Devil's Dictionary: A Guidebook for Cynics, by Ambrose Bierce. ISBN 1-58509-016-6 • 144 pages • 6 x 9 • trade paper • $12.95

The Smoky God: Or The Voyage to the Inner World, by Willis George Emerson. ISBN 1-58509-067-0 • 184 pages • 6 x 9 • trade paper • illustrated • $15.95

A Short History of the World, by H.G. Wells. ISBN 1-58509-211-8 • 320 pages • 6 x 9 • trade paper • $24.95

The Voyages and Discoveries of the Companions of Columbus, by Washington Irving. ISBN 1-58509-500-1 • 352 pages • 6 x 9 • hard cover • $39.95

History of Baalbek, by Michel Alouf. ISBN 1-58509-063-8 • 196 pages • 5 x 8 • trade paper • illustrated • $15.95

Ancient Egyptian Masonry: The Building Craft, by Sommers Clarke and R. Engelback. ISBN 1-58509-059-X • 350 pages • 6 x 9 • trade paper • illustrated • $26.95

That Old Time Religion: The Story of Religious Foundations, by Jordan Maxwell and Paul Tice. ISBN 1-58509-100-6 • 103 pages • 6 x 9 • trade paper • $12.95

The Book of Enoch: A Work of Visionary Revelation and Prophecy, Revealing Divine Secrets and Fantastic Information about Creation, Salvation, Heaven and Hell, translated by R. H. Charles. ISBN 1-58509-019-0 • 152 pages • 5 1/2 x 8 1/2 • trade paper • $13.95

The Book of Enoch: Translated from the Editor's Ethiopic Text and Edited with an Enlarged Introduction, Notes and Indexes, Together with a Reprint of the Greek Fragments, edited by R. H. Charles. ISBN 1-58509-080-8 • 448 pages • 6 x 9 • trade paper • $34.95

The Book of the Secrets of Enoch, translated from the Slavonic by W. R. Morfill. Edited, with Introduction and Notes by R. H. Charles. ISBN 1-58509-020-4 • 148 pages • 5 1/2 x 8 1/2 • trade paper • $13.95

Enuma Elish: The Seven Tablets of Creation, Volume One, by L. W. King. ISBN 1-58509-041-7 • 236 pages • 6 x 9 • trade paper • illustrated • $18.95

Enuma Elish: The Seven Tablets of Creation, Volume Two, by L. W. King. ISBN 1-58509-042-5 • 260 pages • 6 x 9 • trade paper • illustrated • $19.95

Enuma Elish, Volumes One and Two: The Seven Tablets of Creation, by L. W. King. Two volumes from above bound as one. ISBN 1-58509-043-3 • 496 pages • 6 x 9 • trade paper • illustrated • $38.90

The Archko Volume: Documents that Claim Proof to the Life, Death, and Resurrection of Christ, by Drs. McIntosh and Twyman. ISBN 1-58509-082-4 • 248 pages • 6 x 9 • trade paper • $20.95

The Lost Language of Symbolism: An Inquiry into the Origin of Certain Letters, Words, Names, Fairy-Tales, Folklore, and Mythologies, by Harold Bayley. ISBN 1-58509-070-0 • 384 pages • 6 x 9 • trade paper • $27.95

The Book of Jasher: A Suppressed Book that was Removed from the Bible, Referred to in Joshua and Second Samuel, translated by Albinus Alcuin (800 AD). ISBN 1-58509-081-6 • 304 pages • 6 x 9 • trade paper • $24.95

The Bible's Most Embarrassing Moments, with an Introduction by Paul Tice. ISBN 1-58509-025-5 • 172 pages • 5 x 8 • trade paper • $14.95

History of the Cross: The Pagan Origin and Idolatrous Adoption and Worship of the Image, by Henry Dana Ward. ISBN 1-58509-056-5 • 104 pages • 6 x 9 • trade paper • illustrated • $11.95

Was Jesus Influenced by Buddhism? A Comparative Study of the Lives and Thoughts of Gautama and Jesus, by Dwight Goddard. ISBN 1-58509-027-1 • 252 pages • 6 x 9 • trade paper • $19.95

History of the Christian Religion to the Year Two Hundred, by Charles B. Waite. ISBN 1-885395-15-9 • 556 pages • 6 x 9 • hard cover • $25.00

Symbols, Sex, and the Stars, by Ernest Busenbark. ISBN 1-885395-19-1 • 396 pages • 5 1/2 x 8 1/2 • trade paper • $22.95

History of the First Council of Nice: A World's Christian Convention, A.D. 325, by Dean Dudley. ISBN 1-58509-023-9 • 132 pages • 5 1/2 x 8 1/2 • trade paper • $12.95

The World's Sixteen Crucified Saviors, by Kersey Graves. ISBN 1-58509-018-2 • 436 pages • 5 1/2 x 8 1/2 • trade paper • $29.95

NEXUS Magazine offers you all of the information that the mainstream media will not tell you. It is a fascinating magazine out of Australia and has U.S. distribution. The Book Tree encourages you to try them.

(30) An Alternate
Reality

Di's
33) Las Vegas
35) Calamities
53) entrance
for UFOs

UFO
LOCATIONS
35 Greece

Crystals
35

SYMBOLS
58

Alien
Descriptions
21/28/32 (Tall)
greys
51 (mantis) 52 pic.
67) Inter dimensional +
Extra terrestrial

Download
Info
21

All UFOs
25 LIST
29 Shapes

Dreams
27/28-29

23) 1952-1992 UFOs
Blue Book +
Dr. Hynek

55) STAR MAP

Jobs
30

ATOMS
28

Bases
63) D + Mars

LaVergne, TN USA
28 March 2011

221755LV00002B/2/P

9 781585 091355